Self-Publishing
Can Be Profitable
and *Immensely* Rewarding

Self-Publishing Can Be Profitable and *Immensely* Rewarding

By *Ruth Raby Moen*

A Common Sense Approach to Publishing, Promoting, and Marketing Your Own Books.

By: Ruth Raby Moen
Edited by: Paul Cocke

Published by: Snohomish Publishing Company,
                    114 Avenue "C", Snohomish, WA 98290

Distributed by: Flying Swan Publications, PO Box 46,
                    Sedro-Woolley, WA 98284

Library of Congress Catalog Card Number: 95-067353
ISBN: 0-9635653-4-6

It's quite a commitment, writing a book
Somewhat like getting married
It nags at you
Keeps you awake at night
And demands incredible amounts of your time and energy
It sends thrills up your spine when things are going well
And spirals you to the depths of depression when they're not
You sweat, you cry out, and occasionally bawl
Then finally, when it's finished, it leaves you
Satiated and fulfilled
Ready for a long nap, and wishing you hadn't stopped smoking.

By Ruth Raby Moen,
Author of −
DEADLY DECEPTIONS, A Mystery Novel
ONLY ONE WAY OUT, A Mystery
HAYSEEDS IN MY HAIR, A Memoir

TABLE OF CONTENTS

So, you wrote a book. You spent a good part of your life staring at a blank paper or computer screen – waiting, praying, for that inspired quickening that meant your prose would flow from your fingers like a spring stream and any writing you performed would ultimately enlighten the world. When that didn't happen, as it very rarely does, you quietly and with great resolve went to work. Day after day, the plotting, the researching went on. Week after week, you wrote, you rewrote and rewrote again. Delving into a thesaurus for just the right word to shape that phrase or sentence. Calling a friend, a clinic, or a law office for advice and their specialized input. Craving that perfect definition, turn of speech, or metaphor.

Eventually, after much note-taking and many false starts, a book was born. All of the creative-writing classes, the library check-outs and the bookstore haunts have paid off.

Your manuscript is finished.

• I Felt The Need To Write ...

Perhaps it's a simple vignette of true stories about your own life experiences. Or maybe you've done a full genealogical history of your family tree. Many people, who had never really considered themselves writers before, feel that before they leave this world they'd best see that they're remembered in a certain way. These brave souls take up pen and paper for the first time, determined to write a history of themselves and their ancestors for those upcoming grandchildren and great-grandchildren who today are too small to know you well or even those yet to be born.

Take heart. They will one day be very grateful that you took the time to tell them who you were, how you felt about things, and what your life was like. I doubt I could find a single person today who would deny that they'd love to have something left to them from their great-grandmother, say a diary or a book of poems, to pass down through the years and the generations. Or perhaps there is a family member who led an outstanding life and you feel the details of their adventures should be recorded for posterity. If this was your motivation to write and is the main thrust of your manuscript, chances are, this book will be a family keepsake. And as something that will be treasured for many, many years, it deserves to be published by a reputable printer and in a book form. Don't be surprised if, in creating a piece of work about an era and a way of life that no longer exists, you have written a book that many others outside of your own immediate family would enjoy reading as well.

When I first wrote my memoirs, it was only as a means of understanding myself and my life. I also wanted to leave an accurate record of those experiences. But mostly, I wanted my descendants to know the stock from which they came and to leave them with this message: that if Old Granny could have overcome her trials and tribulations, a little the worse for wear but still fully enjoying her life, then no matter what kind of hardships they may face in life after I'm no longer there to protect them, they can do the same.

It's in their genes.

And I don't want them to ever forget it.

So I wrote stories, one after another, about the things I'd experienced as a child. At the time, I'd hoped that after I was gone, my daughters and their families would find them tucked in a drawer and share them.

But after awhile, those stories took on a life of their own. They eventually became a book co-published by Snohomish Publishing Co. and titled, *Hayseeds In My Hair.* To date, that book has been read not only by my family but thousands of others and its popularity continues to increase. But that's where my rewards of writing only begin.

In addition to the money I've made in the sales of that book, there's been another experience I was totally unprepared for and continue to be amazed each time it happens. The feed-back, the many letters and cards I've received from fans and readers has been incredible. They write to tell me how they bought my book, how they read it, passed it around to all their family members, then felt moved to contact me. Sometimes these readers identify with my memoirs in such a way that when they meet me, they want to grasp my hands, tightly, or even hug me, thanking me profusely for 'writing their story.' It has compensated me many times over for the pain I experienced in a difficult childhood.

• But Now I Need To Be Paid

Then there is another type of manuscript, a novel or a non-fiction book, which was purposely written with an eye to being sold. This author now enters into a process of trying to get it published.

You've attended faithfully the conferences and book fairs, the readings and the book signings. You've joined most every book club and followed the sage advice of every professional you could track down.

After countless query letters to agents and publishers, one of them writes back. You might have had to pay them for the privilege but they're interested and want to see it. Finally, that great moment has arrived. Your talents will be acknowledged.

And ... you stand a chance to be published.

Full of expectations and hope, the manuscript is mailed to their office.

Now comes the waiting. For the next many months, with your life seemingly put on hold, you anxiously await their reply. All the while, what had previously been a simple function of life, such as the ringing of the phone or the arrival of the mail, has now become a major event.

You answer, breathlessly, the phone on the first ring. Fly to the mailbox as the little white truck marked Postal Service rounds the corner. And each day, you feverishly paw through the stack of bills and advertisements, looking for that one precious letter. The one that says the manuscript has been accepted.

That your dream has come true.

That you're going to be published and paid for it.

Eventually, the waiting becomes more than one mortal being can bear. You begin to hound the mailman, "Is that all for today? Is all the mail out?" He nods and waves, and you retreat. Resigned to wait yet another day, another week.

Unable to sleep, you pace the floor at night – worrying, wondering ... *"Have they read it yet? Will they like it?"*

That agent you met at the conference should have called by now. Baffled but still not ready to admit defeat, you check the answering machine – convinced that it hasn't picked up all of the calls it should have.

Finally, months later when you've all but given up, the manuscript is returned. With it, instead of an acceptance letter, you find a filled-in form or a scribbled note stating their regrets.

"Sorry. We're not accepting any new clients at this time."

Awash in disappointment and frustration, you're left wondering if you really do have the stamina to try, try again and doubting whether they read past the first page.

Your precious book.

Your baby.

That extension of yourself that would have ... that really should have been ...

But you've worked too hard. It's too important. You deserve more, the manuscript deserves more than that. In fact, just the writing of it made the phrase, *open a vein and let the words pour forth,* a daily occurrence.

You can't quit now.

So again, and again, that query letter is rewritten and sent out. And again and again, that manuscript is mailed. You wait, you pray, only to see it rejected and returned – over and over again.

No dice.

No one wants it.

Of course, intellectually we all know that the publishing world is a volatile place and hard to crack for any unpublished writer. We all understand that most of the promotional dollars go to established authors and the rest, if lucky enough to get published, get peanuts. And we've all heard, time and time again, that we should never take these rejections personally. But knowing all this doesn't help a whole lot and it certainly doesn't make it feel any better.

So, weary and broken-hearted, you toss the last copy into the closet and slam the door. Enough is enough. Goodbye to the whole darn racket.

Now what? Does this mean goodbye to your dreams, too? To the idea that you'll someday be an author and your books will be available to the general public?

It doesn't have to. It doesn't even mean that you won't be paid for them.

There is another way. A better way.

Consider publishing that book, yourself.

Is it hard? Too complicated? Too expensive? Will a printing bill for thousands of dollars thwart those dreams too?

Not necessarily.

There is a way to get around each one of these hurdles. As you'll see, this is a step-by-step plan by which you can be published and get paid for it. And if you work hard enough at it, be paid *very well*. Best of all, you'll do it *without* being a part of the hassle of the regular channels of publishing.

• CHAPTER ONE •

GETTING STARTED

Plan Ahead But Watch Your Back

• Motivation

It's a good idea, I believe, to determine just exactly *why* you are self-publishing. Are you "testing" the business of publishing? Looking to see if you might want to publish yet another book if this one does well? Or, will this venture into the book-publishing world be a one-time shot *only* for a particular story?

Kathleen Walsh Packard, *(Fling Old Glory, The Story of Patrick Walsh, An Irish-American Fire Chief)*, wrote her book as a loving tribute to her grandfather, Patrick Walsh, an Irish-American immigrant who had been the New York City Fire Commissioner under Mayor LaGuardia in the 1940s.

When Kathleen's mother died at the age of 85, she found herself faced with the prospect of cleaning out her mother's belongings. Included in her mother's things was a suitcase under the bed. That suitcase contained stacks of newspaper clippings of Kathleen's grandfather.

Kathleen promptly went to work, writing his story with the objective of preserving the memory of her grandfather and his accomplishments. Naturally, this was a project that required Kathleen to self-publish.

But Kathleen was soon met with yet another surprise. It seems that the members of her family were not the only ones who are enjoying this book. I quote from a portion of her letter:

"Through my distribution to the fire department network, I was put in contact with The Fire Buff House Publishers which offered to bring my book out in paperback at no expense to myself. Apparently, in addition to officially organized fire departments, there is a sizeable contingent of people across the country who consider themselves fire buffs and take interest in all aspects of firefighting activities. The Fire Buff House Publishers printed 3000 paperbacks in the spring of 1993, of which 1000 have been sold to date, two dollars on each book having been returned to me in royalties."

My story is a little different from Kathleen's. When I first conceived of the idea of being a published author, I did all the things most every aspiring author is told to do.

I wrote and mailed one sparkling query letter after another to every agent and publisher who dared to allow their name and address to be found. I attended the writing conferences as one possessed, not to mention the retreats, the hangouts, and the readings. All in the hope of finding a publisher who would show an interest in my work.

I bought and read reams of books and schmoozed up a storm at every opportunity. Talk about perseverance! And although I made a few friends with some other author wannabees, none of the work or the expenses (I shudder to think of all that wasted postage) did me one bit of good. My work was rejected at every turn.

My last hope was to self-publish. But, as Kathleen and I both learned and as the rest of you will also discover, there are a certain number of must-dos before you go to print.

• Bookkeeping

Have a system of bookkeeping set up or at least a good understanding of how it is done. If you feel you need some help in this regard, contact your local Community College for workshops and classes on business management. Many areas have a local Small Business Administration Office set up to give informative and inexpensive workshops, including free personal consultations and advice on a broad range of subjects, including taxes, loans, and accounting. Look for these in your area phone book or use this address to find the branch nearest you:

Small Business Administration
409 3rd St SW
Washington D.C. 20416
1-800-827-5722

• Company Name

As a going business concern, you'll want to look as professional as possible. You are now a small press publisher and it's important to separate your name, or at least the name you write under, from the name of your business. As this name will be the trademark by which your books will be identified, you'll want one which will distinguish your books from any others yet somehow relate to you and your style of writing. For instance, a book on economics or banking would be wise if marketed under a company name that sounds conservative. Like it might be mentioned in the *Wall Street Journal*.

On the other hand, this same name should never promote a children's book. That doesn't mean that you could not publish and promote both books. Just have a different company name for each. Make sure you're not using the same name as some other publisher by checking it with your local library.

I named my company, *Flying Swan Publications*, for the Trumpeter Swans that migrate from Alaska to winter here in the stubble corn fields of Skagit Valley in Washington State. As these mighty birds take wing with their long necks thrust out before them, they give off a cacophony of wild and haunting honks. These thrilling sounds have more than once sent me sailing to the window or the yard – watching as flock after flock passed over our house. Flying low and in a perfect V formation.

• Logo

Your company logo should also take some thought. It should be simple enough that it can be reduced in size and still be recognizable on a letterhead or business card, yet symbolize at first glance your company name. Most print shops have reams of clip art, there for anyone's use. If they don't have what you're looking for, try a good graphic artist. They can do wonders with a simple sketch or even a snapshot. Again, this represents your book and, indirectly, yourself. Don't be afraid to put some personality in it.

• P.O. Box

You'll also need a Post Office box if you don't already have one. Besides looking more professional, it will afford you the privacy we all need in a fatally-flawed world. Later on in the marketing section of this book is more information on the use of the P.O. Box and the Post Office itself.

• Bank Accounts

Set up a business bank account, separate from your personal account, using your company name. It will prove invaluable at bookkeeping time or when applying for credit. If the funds are running low for business expenditures, rather than pay bills with your personal account, simply make a "loan" to your business with a deposit from one account to the other.

• Business Cards and Stationary

Imprinted with your P.O. address and logo, business cards and stationary are another must. Consider a business letter, especially one to whom you hope to sell some books, as your salesman or agent. It will make that terribly important, first impression of you, your company, and your books. We've all had to learn to dress in suits and have our hair styled for an upcoming job interview. No matter what your talents and experience, you'd best look good when you meet that interviewer or you might as well stay home. Conversely, a letter banged out on plain computer paper – fraught with spelling and grammatical errors – has the same chance of selling books as the unshaven bum in raggedly jeans has of being hired. Also, you'll want to consider bookmarks and mailing labels – if not now, at least later on.

• Business Licenses

If you don't already have a business license with your city, county, and state governments, get one. Your local City Hall or county courthouse can help you with most of the requirements. Be sure to list each company name you plan to use. If you later add another name, simply notify the license department.

Be sure to ask for information on how to apply for a *Tax Identification Number* with the Department of Revenue or look them up in the phone book. You must have this before you can sell your books directly to your customers at retail price. They will send you a packet that explains the correct amount of sales tax to charge, how and when that tax money is to be turned over to their agency, and the forms with which to do it. It will be your responsibility to keep an accounting of how much tax money you've collected and be prepared to turn that money over to them at the correct time. They are usually quite helpful with answering your questions as to their requirements.

• ISBN

You must have an ISBN (International Standard Book Number) *printed* on the back cover of every book if you want to be taken seriously by most bookstores, wholesalers, and distributors. They will need these numbers to stock, to sell, and to keep track of inventory. To apply for a list of ISBN numbers, call, fax, or send a letter to:

R.R. Bowker
121 Chanlon Rd
New Providence, New Jersey 07974
908-665-6770, FAX: 908-464-3553.

There's no charge for the list but you will be charged a handling fee of $100. For this fee, you will be sent a list of ISBN numbers, instructions on how to use them and the forms. These are ABI (Advanced Book Information) forms. Each time you have a book ready to print, first select one ISBN number, fill in the ABI form and send it back to Bowker. This process will get your book listed in their publication, *Books In Print*. Keep in mind, that this is a valuable service, since this publication is used as reference material throughout the country by libraries, distributors, wholesalers, bookstores and interested individuals.

• Bar Codes

Sometimes referred to as Bookland EAN, these are also essential. This is the way the ISBN is used, as referred to in the above paragraph. The title and price, when given to the printer along with the manuscript, are printed directly onto the back cover with magnetic ink. In a highly computerized world, almost any product, including books, will have them. These are used not only by the price scanners at the check-out counter but also as a convenient way for that store to know which books are selling, how many are in stock, and when to reorder. More and more, the bookstores, the grocery stores and even the distributors will think twice before ordering any book without them as most of their accounting systems are no longer set up to handle anything that requires a hand entry.

Two companies that I have dealt with quite successfully are:

Data-Index
PO Box 500
Kirkland, WA 98083-0500
800-426-2183, FAX: 206-885-2467

and

Fotel GGX
11 Middle Neck Road
Great Neck, N.Y., 11021
516-487-6370, FAX: 516-487-6449

• Copyright Protection

Important, yes. But not as complicated as one might think. The section below has been taken, verbatim, from the pamphlet produced by the Copyright Office of the Library of Congress:

"Copyright protection subsists from the time the work is created in fixed form; that is, it is an incident of the process of authorship.

The copyright in the work of authorship immediately becomes the property of the author who created it."

Therefore, a copyright is secured automatically when the work is created. But it never hurts to give notice that this piece of work is indeed copyrighted, especially if it leaves your hands for any length of time such as when a manuscript is being mailed out or even handed to another person to be read.

The legal form of notice of copyright is to show the copyright symbol (the letter 'C') or the word 'copyright' on the created work in an obvious location, along with the year date and the name of the owner of the copyright.

Example: Copyright 1995 Ruth Raby Moen

A copyright can then be *registered* as a legal formality, which makes a public record of the copyright and protects the owner against infringement. This registration is necessary before an infringement suit can be filed in court.

The forms and the instructions for registering can be had simply by requesting them in writing from:

> Registration of Copyrights
> Library of Congress
> Washington DC, 20559

To register your copyright, send a completed application form, a nonrefundable filing fee of $20, and a nonreturnable deposit of the work being registered. If the work is unpublished, send one complete copy of the manuscript. If the work is already published, send two complete copies.

• Copyright and Publication Dates

That first year of the copyright date and the publication date might be the only year your book will be considered a viable commodity by bookstores and distributors. Unless your book becomes an instant and huge success, most bookstores – especially the chain stores – won't be willing to carry it on their shelves for more than six months *within the year of the copyright or publication date* before they send it back and replace it with something even newer.

Don't be misled – your book can be marketed for as long as you're willing to keep it in print. But after that first year is up, it will no longer be *just-out*. And whether you consider that important or not, they will.

Note: The copyright year should be the actual year you published this work or that you intend to publish this work. After September of any given year, if the copies of the book are not yet ready to go out into the marketplace, most publishers use the following year date for their copyright date. It will take that long before the copies are available to the buying public.

You'll also need a publication date but, here again, you'll need to plan ahead. It will need to be in the same year or early the next year as the copyright date. In order to get the most exposure, it's not necessary to use the same date your book becomes available to the reading public – if you find yourself too close to the end of that year. Even before the shipment arrives from the printer, you'll need time to send the galleys to certain review magazines and to distributors for advance sales. The size of their order will help you determine how large your first print run should be, and help you get the most out of that first year.

I usually try to have my books printed and ready to ship to the distributors by August of any given year and have the publication date set for January of the following year. That gives me the ability to show them at the fall trade shows in September, October and November as a brand-new, hot-off-the-press peek at next year's titles and still be able to offer them at the following year's spring shows as something new. (For more information, see Chapter Five, Trade Shows and Conventions.)

• The Library of Congress CIP Program Versus the PCN Program

Basically, the biggest difference between these two programs is that the Cataloging in Publication program (CIP) does NOT include books paid for or subsidized by individual authors or books published by a house publishing the works of only one author. In other words, the works of a self-published author.

Not so, with the Preassigned Card Number program (PCN). It *does* include self-published works, paid for or subsidized by individual authors or a house publishing the works of only one author.

Therefore, if you intend to self-publish your own work, you should apply to the Library of Congress for a Preassigned Library of Congress Catalog Card Number (PCN), *before* the manuscript is published. This is a free service and essential when selling your book to libraries. This is their numbering system, as opposed to the ISBN. Any book without it, even if it has been donated, will have to be carded by hand before it can be placed on a shelf. Send your request in writing to:

Library of Congress
Cataloging in Publication Division
Washington, DC 20540
(202) 707-9797

· CHAPTER TWO ·

If having a book published were to be considered a simile to giving birth to a baby, and the writing of that book was seen as the gestation period, this next part should be regarded as the labor pains. For some reason I can't readily explain, there is an emotional tide that sweeps an author at about this point, unexpected and overwhelming. It's tough to get through, even painful at times, but one which will give you an incredible sense of accomplishment once it's resolved.

· Editing

A friend of mine and an excellent editor, *Michael Barrett*, has explained his duties far better than I ever could. The following is what he has to say about it.

"When editors breeze through forty pages in a hour or eight hundred in a week, I worry that they have not undergone the agonies prerequisite to launching someone's words into eternity. I begin to ask annoying questions:

Have they weighed every phrase and sentence of the script to determine whether the author's meaning will be carried to the intended audience?

Have they measured every revision they propose to make against the advantages of the author's original voice and presentation?

Have they pondered the effectiveness of every phrase to the limits of their grammatical ear – and then beyond, with two or three modern-usage guides at hand?

Have they strained their eyes for typos and transpositions, especially in those parts of the manuscript retyped or reorganized? Have they edited and proofread their own editing as well?

Have they – or the proofreaders whose work they manage – groveled in the details of the footnotes, tables, and appendices until every last em-dash, and subscript is marked, every parenthesis is closed, and all abbreviations and italicizations are consistent?

Have they cast a legal eye upon every quoted phrase, defamatory comment, trade name, allegation, and attribution, whether it appears in

9

footnote, caption, dedication, title page, or main text?

Have they stepped back to consider the impact of the whole as well as the parts, tuned an ear to overtones of sexism, racism, ageism, ethnocentrism, and any other isms that will undermine the intentions of author and publisher or unintentionally alienate the reader?

Have they, if required, provided all the editorial embellishments to the text-title, subtitle, subheads, author notes, editorial notes, sidebars, blowups, dingbats, and instructions to the designer?

Have they, if it is the policy of the publication, cleared every significant revision and addition with the author?

Editors who can do all this in a twinkling are either in league with the devil or as one with the gods".

– *Michael Barrett, Editor*
Business Pulse & Apropos Magazines

Michael also moonlights as an editor for writers and self-publishers. His address, and some other editors who also do an excellent job at very reasonable rates, are:

Michael S. Barrett
301 Haines Street
Sedro-Woolley, WA 98284
360-855-1127

Miriam Stratton
Rt. 2 box 846
Pullman, WA 99163

And last but not least, let me **highly** recommend the editor of this book, *Paul Cocke*. Paul is not only an old hand at editing, having been a reporter, copy editor, and assistant state editor for a large newspaper, he also has a great deal of experience at ghost-writing, creating news or press releases, advertising copy and/or newsletters.

Paul Cocke
1009 Fidalgo Street
Sedro-Woolley, WA 98284
360-855-2330

As the above text points out, enough cannot be said about the importance of having professionally-edited copy. It's difficult at best, if not impossible, for an author to edit his/her own writing. Your best bet is to give that manuscript your best shot, then find a professional to point out all those erroneous places that evaded you. Whether by friends who just happen to be editors or by someone who makes their living that way, be sure to have at least one go through your manuscript word by word – red pen at the ready – eliminating each over-worked cliche, misspelled word and worn-out comma.

In addition to the names I've offered above, an obvious place to look for an editor is at your local newspaper or magazine office. Many times, they're willing to do some moonlighting for very reasonable rates. Also, the local community college or even high school English classes can be harboring an experienced editor. Don't count them out. Even the pros in this business find it necessary to pay their mortgage with a steady paycheck.

You'll also want to find someone who can critique your manuscript. Sometimes called 'book doctors,' you'll need someone who can point out the weaknesses in the story itself. Places where a point you've been trying to make does not quite come across, either by not enough description or because of a convoluted sentence that gets the reader lost in its verbiage. Or, sometimes just the opposite is at work. By trying to make yourself clear, you've filled up a page or two with philosophical thoughts which you, awakened from a dream at three o'clock in the morning, thought to be wise and decisive. Naturally, as the author, you know what it means. But in the glaring light of day, that prose that felt so right – when seen on paper and in the middle of the story – only serves to break up the action and confuse the reader.

Even the most experienced writers cannot always critique their own work. Therefore, it's best to let someone else find all the faults. *Be aware that a critiqueing service is not necessarily the same thing as editing!* Although these persons may also be experienced and talented editors, do not take it for granted as this may not be the case.

• Book Covers

"You cannot worry too much or spend enough time with an artist or graphic artist, working on the cover. It is the first thing a reader sees and determines whether or not they pick it up. It is therefore, absolutely critical that the cover is done in a way that the reader is drawn into the story even before they crack the first page."
– Miriam Uhlig, Killing Time Mystery Books

There's no getting around basic facts. People buy books for different reasons. Many times, and especially for the hard-core bookstore-browser, any new book by a popular author, especially one who's attained the distinction of having had a bestseller, is snatched from the shelves before it can acquire its first speck of dust. That cover could have

11

been cut from an old paper bag, and the truly loyal fans could care less. But an unknown author trying to scratch a niche in the book-buying business needs all the help they can get. In this very competitive, appearance-conscious world, it's time to put your creativity to the test.

Who knows best what that book is about? Who else has been expected to condense the essence of that story, on a minute's notice, into one or two sentences on demand? Formed those word-pictures in people's minds? Written those query letters and synopses and jacket blurbs and hyped promotional pieces? Almost always, and unless a friend can be found or a publicist hired, the answer to all these questions remains with the author.

Therefore, have something in mind when you visit that graphics artist. Don't just turn over the manuscript with the parting request, *"Make it look intriguing. Something classy"*. If you're lucky, they might have time to read the manuscript, but most won't. Make a sketch. Work with them. Take that picture in your mind and draw it out. No matter how preliminary or crude, give them as much to go on as you can.

Be sure to tell them you'll want to see a blueline – which is a preliminary copy of the cover which has not yet gone to print. This is your last chance to make corrections or additions, or even to throw the whole thing out and start anew. Most printing shops will offer that as a service anyway, but just in case they get in a hurry, be sure to leave instructions. And don't forget to take that synopsis and jacket blurb with you.

Note: You'll need all the extra book covers you can get, for promotional purposes. Be sure to order extra ones from the printer.

• Price

By the time you've come this far, you've probably already made some decisions that will affect the price of your book. How big is it? How attractive is the front cover? Does the back cover have the much-needed bar codes? Research other newly-published books in the same genre but not necessarily by a famous person or author. How are they selling? Here again, make sure you're not comparing apples with oranges.

You'll never be able to compete with the mass paperback publishers. Don't even try. Their print orders are so huge it would stagger the imagination of the average self-publisher, but it gets the price of each copy WAY down there. Trade paperback size (5.25 X 8) usually sells for more, even though it is the same book. The customers seem to feel that since they're holding something 'larger,' or a little 'out of the norm' they're more willing to pay that slightly higher price.

Don't make the same mistake as some others by having the expenses – the graphic artists, the printers, the fees and the postage – the single most influence on the price you set for your book. Perhaps your book winds up costing you $2 to $3 apiece, or even $5, by the time you consider everything. $50 here, $50 there. After awhile, it really begins to add up. And if you add in a profit margin, it all hikes that price up even higher.

Forget it. Your book is worth no more than what an average buyer is willing to pay. No more, and no less. Remember, a consumer might pay $20 or even $25 for a new, just-released hardback novel by their favorite author. But if you're writing fiction as an unknown author, I'd advise you not to go over $9.95 or $12.95 at the most if you're publishing fiction. Unless your book is running 500 pages or more. That changes things too, including the look and the worth. Nonfiction generally sells for a little more, as a consumer is motivated to buy for different reasons.

• Selecting a Printer

Here's where the friendship with the neighborhood weekly newspaper comes in handy. As with many other writers who first approach a printer, I was met with an estimate of thousands of dollars. I didn't have thousands of dollars to spend on a book. I'd already spent too much on my writing and felt I'd gotten nothing for it.

What to do now?

Thank goodness, I had sown a few friendly seeds at the local newspaper office. Actually, I had worked there part time, as a journalist. No, I wasn't paid much but I had felt the exposure and the experience was worth it. I was right. Come to find out, this particular newspaper is owned by the same man who owns a print shop. Voila!

Now I had someone with whom I could talk. Someone who knew me. Yes, that estimate for a print run still cost in the thousands but he was willing to work with me. I ended up paying him in payments and out of the proceeds of the book sales itself. That particular man is *Ed Wise, (or his son, Jeff Wise,) from Snohomish Publishing, 114 Avenue 'C', Snohomish, Washington, 98290, (360) 568-1242.* And, incidentally, he's the publisher of this book. Without his initial help, I sincerely doubt that any one of my manuscripts would ever have been seen in print.

By the way, I highly suggest you give this company a call before you make that final decision on who you want to do your printing. They're fair, they're professional, reasonably priced, and they'll produce a nice-looking book for you including the layout.

13

Some other printers you might contact for a comparable quote are the following companies:

BookMasters, Inc.
638 Jefferson St.
PO Box 159
Ashland, Ohio 44805
800-537-6727, Fax: 419-281-1731
800-622-9256

Amica International
1201 First Ave. S. Stuite 203
Seattle, WA 98134
206-467-1035, Fax: 206-467-1522

Gilliland Printing, Inc.
215 North Summit
Arkansas City, Kansas 67005
316-442-0500, Fax: 316-442-8504
800-332-8200

Note: When ordering an estimate, ask for a quote on quantities of 300, 500, 1000, 2500, and 5000 copies. And when comparing estimates between different companies, be sure to compare apples with apples and not oranges, ie; 500 to 500, 1000 to 1000, etc. Also, how itemized is their estimate for other services? Ask them if their price includes layout and shipping costs.

• Determining The Size of a Print Run

How many copies should you order? That depends on a lot of things, but mostly on how well you can get it out there and how well it'll sell. The type of book you're publishing, your commitment to marketing the book, and your budget are just three of the considerations you'll want to study. This is a personal decision, but one thing is for certain: It doesn't hurt to order a smaller print run in the beginning, (from 500 to 1000 is considered a small run). You can always have another print-run after the distributors and bookstores are on line and those orders begin to come in. And that will probably take awhile.

• Loans, Bartering, Horse-trading, and Other Fiscal Matters

The parties over and it's time to pick up the tab. Hopefully, you either have a nice, cushiony savings account or you've already made other arrangements. Believe it or not, rather than paying cash up front, there are other options.

• SBA Loans

If you're considering a loan, the Small Business Administration might be the first place you'll want to go. As mentioned before, they can be extremely helpful – especially if you ask for counseling with a SCORE (Service Corps of Retired Executives) Volunteer. They'll help you fill out the forms for an SBA loan and, when asked, can offer quite valuable advice on most any business topic. And their services are free.

SCORE Volunteers are women and men who represent all walks of business life, as former or active accountants, business owners, corporation executives, lawyers, etc. who are dedicated to helping all business owners realize their entrepreneurial dreams. You can usually contact them through the local Small Business Administration office or write to them at:

National SCORE Office
409 Third St., SW, Suite 5900
Washington, DC 20024
Or call (202) 205-6762

• Just Say "Charge it"

Also, most printers have charge-card services. Or some of them will even carry your loan on their own books – especially if they already know you. Be sure to make these arrangements well in advance of the delivery date of your books.

• Bartering

Whatever happened to the old-fashioned horse-trader? There was a time in this country when a pregnant mare could be swapped for a good chunk of land, a few colored beads and a hand mirror were sufficient payment for enough beaver pelts to make a great winter coat, and a small herd of sheep could actually purchase a new bride!

Well, I have news for you, folks. This is still America and you can still make any kind of arrangements you want, to pay for anything you owe. You can write it up in a contract or simply shake hands, as long as the other party agrees and as long as it's legal.

We are writers – thinkers, philosophers, and reasoning people. Take a little of that wonderful ability to create – a tiny seed – plant it in a field of resourceful ingenuity, and all sorts of ideas will begin to bloom.

• Work For Hire

That printer is a business person. With all sorts of business-related necessities that are normally provided by others such as employees, ordered from a service, or simply purchased off a shelf. Talk to them. Find out what their needs are and figure a way to fill one or two of them. Do they need advertising copy from time to time? Someone to make up fliers? Put together a sample brochure or pamphlet for a prospective printing company and make your pitch. All they can do is say "No, thanks." They can't chop you up in pieces and feed you to the hogs. And who knows? They might even like it.

Maybe they've been looking for a salesman. Or someone to do some typesetting – or graphics work – or drive a truck. Anything that will pay off your debt.

Also, find out who the parent company is for any other local publishing companies, including the neighborhood weeklies. They're always needing writers. And they just might own a print shop.

• Joint Ventures and Partnerships

Another often overlooked asset is the manuscript itself – a valuable commodity whose ownership can be shared much like any other business. And here again, the possibilities are limitless.

Perhaps your printer wouldn't mind printing the manuscript themselves if they were the owner of the publishing rights. And perhaps you could have exclusive rights to the marketing. Or you can share in those rights, with each of you getting what you really want out of the deal. The printer needs to be paid for the printing costs and you need to be published.

Negotiate. Give a little – and take a little. You can both get what you really want, if you're both willing to talk about it.

• CHAPTER THREE •

DESK-TOP PUBLISHING

Warning: This next chapter contains enough technical lingo and computer-related gibberish to place the less-experienced user in severe danger of feeling so intimidated they can't go on. Seized with whimpering fits of indecision.
This is not good.
But for those brave pioneers who want to know the ins and outs of this complicated computer world, I have included a partial list of the most popular PC's and their software pertaining to the publishing industry. Hopefully, you will find it a handy guide. The others have three choices, as I see it:
1. Consider it a learning experience.
2. Take it shopping ... to the computer store.
3. This step depends on your personal experience and preferences.

• Computers

Perhaps you're a computer whiz who could do quantum leaps beyond my limited understanding of computereeze. If so, then this has no bearing whatsoever on your case. Or, last of all, for those pencil-and-legal-pad die-hards who still write their stories out in longhand and shrink in horror at the thought of creating their prose on a machine, turn directly to Chapter 4 and forget you ever saw this part.

Remember, if you don't have a lot of expensive computers and programs, all is not lost. Your manuscript can still be processed. It may not have been written on a word-processor – or if it was, maybe it's the wrong type to integrate into the commercial printers' programs. Say, at the time, all you had was an old typewriter and a burning desire to write.

No problem. Simply deliver that manuscript written or typed out on paper. Make sure it's not your only copy. One of their employees will type it into their program for you. Yes, it will cost you more but we all do what we have to do at the time. You'll have a chance to go over it later for errors. This is what a blue-line is for.

Note: Be sure to inform the commercial printer that this service will be necessary so that he/she can reserve the extra time it will take and figure it into the estimate.

• Computers and the Self-Published Author

The computer and software industries have revolutionized the self-publishing market. These industries have melded hardware with software to produce machines capable of providing a self-published author with 'camera-ready' artwork. 'Camera-ready' means that the text has been prepared and set – much like the clear, black and white original you would use on a copy machine for running off multiple copies.

These are then ready for the print-run, which will ultimately become the pages of your book. At that time, you'll be given a 'blue-line' from the printer. A 'blue-line' is a light copy of those pages, printed on cheap paper with watered-down ink.

This will be your last chance to make any changes. Careful, though. Should you suddenly find more than one or two places where more editing is necessary, it can run into a little money as each change in the text means that the whole page must be re-set. And if the changes are large enough to affect the following pages, you'll end up paying for a re-set for each one of those pages. Be sure you are aware of exactly how much that printer will charge for a re-set on a blue-line.

Desktop publishing software saves money and time by keeping the self-publisher from having to deal with editing in the blue-line. The proof and editing of a manuscript takes place at home, *before* it goes to the commercial printer. No more proofing blue-line copies means less out-of-pocket expenses when it comes time to pay the printer.

The physical formatting that is required for 'Camera Ready' copy can be identified by calling the commercial printer and asking what size image area is needed. In fact, this can be done at the same time you ask them for an estimate. The remainder of the process is identified by the type of computer software and output device. In other words, if you intend to deliver the manuscript on a disc, they'll need to know what kind of word processor you used. If it's not compatible with their software, they'll need change it.

The DTP (Desktop Publishing) arena is dominated by two types of PCs (Personal Computers): IBM's or their compatibles, and MacIntoshes. These machines have many software packages that will assist an author in preparing their manuscript. It could be a word processing package such as Wordperfect or Word for Windows or high end DTP packages like Quark Express or PageMaker. The primary purpose of the DTP for a self-publishing author is to produce Camera Ready Art (CRA) or output.

IBM compatibles are the most common machine for an author due to its low cost and readily available components. The base machine should be at least a 386-33 mhz with 2 mb of RAM, and 80+ mb Hard drive. There should be a 3.5" or 5.25" floppy drive so that you can output your files to a diskette for transfer to the commercial printer. There are numerous brand name manufacturers of quality PC components. Most computer stores should have them in stock or at least on order. The price for a complete system varies from $800 for a 386 to $2,300 for a high end 486 system.

The MacIntosh machines are another platform that is used in the printing world. Graphic design is the strong point for these machines but you will find them more than adequate for book publishing. The MacIntoshs range from $1,000 to $4,500 and are usually offered as complete systems. Check with a local MacIntosh dealer.

Software to produce CRA are numerous, but the largest packages for the IBM and MacIntosh are PageMaker 5.0, Ventura Publisher, and Quark Express. These are the more flexible programs allowing the widest variety of graphics and text importation. They are considered high priced at the $450 to $800 range. There are other vendors that are considered middle ground, such a Page Publisher, and Envision Publisher. These are significantly lower in cost but lack some of the graphic features you'll find in the more expensive packages.

I have been concentrating on some of the more popular DTP programs on the market today. But most word processors may be used as well since the critical component is the printing device. As long as the image area on the page matches what your commercial printer needs, you'll only need to check the printed output.

The quality of the work produced will determine what printing device you need. Typically, a 300 dpi (dots per inch) printer will output printable matter that is considered of average quality, (sometimes called 'letter quality'). The higher the dpi, the superior the output. This type of printer will usually be a laser printer which uses toner to apply the 'ink' to the paper – much like a copy machine. The computer images the page like a snapshot is processed from film and then sends the page output to the printer. This yields an extremely accurate font with a crisply clear output.

When comparing laser printers you will find two terms being associated with them, *Postscript and PCL*. Either term describes a font language that builds the font accurately and allows interpretation by the printer. *Postscript* is common in the printing industry as a standard. Most service bureaus or output houses accept *Postscript* which makes getting high quality output relatively easy. The cost for a good home/office use laser printer is around $600. Laser printers will typically work with both of the platforms mentioned above.

Note: There are stores which offer computers and their software at reduced or even wholesale prices. Check *Office Depot, Costco,* or any of the other large warehouse stores before you buy. Even *Amway* offers some very good deals at reduced prices.

Computers for Desktop Publishing

I. IBM compatibles
   A. Hardware
      1. Minimum requirements
         (a) 386-33 mhz with 2 mb RAM, 80+ mb HD
         (b) Printer – 300 dpi laser or ink jet
      2. High end requirements
         (a) 486 or Pentium w/8-32 mb RAM, 550+ mb HD
         (b) Printer – 1200 dpi laser
   B. Software
      1. PageMaker 5.0
         (a) Price range $550.00
      2. Ventura Publisher
         (a) Price range $450.00
      3. Page Publisher
         (a) Price range $69.00
      4. Envision Publisher
         (a) Price range $75.00

II. MacIntosh and compatibles
   A. Hardware
      1. Minimum requirements
         (a) Mac Ci, 68030, 4 mb, 100+ mb HD
         (b) Price Range $800.00 - $1200.00
      2. High end requirements
         (a) PowerPC 7100, 16mb, 550+mb HD
         (b) Price range $3500.00
   B. Software
      1. PageMaker 5.0
         (a) Price range $600.00

2. Quark Express
    (a) Price range $600.00
3. Home Publisher
    (a) Price range $99.00
4. First Publisher
    (a) Price range $75.00

Note: This is not a complete list of programs or computers by any means. It is, I am told, a list of the more widely-used models. For a more comprehensive catalog, call or visit your local computer store or representative.

• CHAPTER FOUR •

MARKETING

• Don't Quit Your Day Job Yet

In order to have a ghost of a chance at success, you must know or at least have reasonable confidence that once printed you can sell those copies. Let me put it another way. You can't afford to pay the printer if you don't have a plan as to how you're going to market those books.

As with any other business, you need a marketing plan. And I suggest you write it out, month by month and dollar by dollar – just what you plan to do, what you can afford to do, and how it fits into your budget. Don't forget, within a few months of the book's release, there will be an income that will be added to that budget.

This does not necessarily mean a lot of expensive advertising. In fact, you need not invest in any paid advertising at all. It does mean some hard, dedicated work with focus and with foresight. This chapter is dedicated to the promotion and marketing of that book, successfully. It is basically my own plan and one which has worked quite well for me.

I believe strongly in working with a combination of press releases, reviews, direct mail, wholesalers/distributors, networking, and personal appearances. So, let us begin at the beginning.

By now, you should have already selected a printer, and delivered that manuscript. But don't stop there – don't even slow down. There are a number of things you'll want to do to get some of those books sold and it's best to do as much as you can, NOW. Before the books arrive. Once that delivery is made and your garage or closets and most of your hallways are stacked chin-high with cases of books, it's awfully nice to have a fistful of orders to back them up.

• The Press Kit

Elaine Feldman has been a publicist and a director of marketing for a number of years. She sees a well-organized press kit as an invaluable aid and promotional tool in any writing career. Her book, and one which I highly recommend, *The Writer's Guide to Self-Promotion and Public-*

ity, (Para Publishing, PO Box 4232-175, Santa Barbara, CA 93140-4232, (800) PARAPUB), elaborates on this theory.

"In undertaking self-promotion, there are things you must do before you do anything else. To be taken seriously you have to present yourself as a professional. It is, therefore, vital that you assemble a personal press kit."

— *Elaine Feldman*

I whole-heartedly agree. You will be expected by those contacts with whom you'll be working not only to have an informative and professional-looking press kit, but to keep it updated.

You'll want to include a background sheet, printed on your office stationary. This is not a resume, in that you can exclude any information which does not directly pertain to your writing career and the accomplishments you've made. These can include a mention of any publications you've been published in or have written for publication. If there are quite a few of them, simply state the amount and list only those that are relevant. Also, list any awards or you've won or honors you've received. If you are considered an expert in the same field as the book you are promoting, be sure to list how and any verification.

Be sure to have photocopies of all you've listed – other than that which is too bulky – such as a book. In that instance, have ready an extra book cover or a clean copy of the book cover.

Many believe a professional-quality photograph is an important part of any press kit. This is true especially if you intend to set up personal or TV appearances.

Next, you will need a press kit folder. Naturally, the best kind would be one which features your book cover on the front panel. If you cannot afford to have this done by the printer, you can make up your own. Purchase a supply of inexpensive, plain colored and pocketed folders at your local office supply. Then, simply glue an extra book cover on the front.

Inside this folder, place one copy of each article, review and award, mentioned above – the best and most recent ones first. Also, your photograph. Put the background sheet on top. Don't forget to place your business card in the slats if the folder has one or adhered to the pocket with a paper clip.

• News Or Press Releases

These should be started on even before the book comes back from the printer. Especially then, as you'll be swamped for awhile once the book is ready for the marketplace.

A good news or press release should read like a well-written article.

Engage the reader. Make it personal. What could this book mean to *them*? How could it, in the case of a non-fiction, inform them and ultimately affect *their* lives? If you've written a set of poems, are they so enlightening and moving that this book will change forever, even in a small way, the perception a reader might have of life? Or, in the case of a novel, does it simply promise to entertain and to keep them perched on the edge of their seats with suspense?

Find the hook and condense it down to a headline in bold type of three to seven words. Add a few more lines to describe the story and build some interest. Always keep them double-spaced if not triple and add the pertinent information at the bottom – i.e. publication date, book size, ISBN, and the number of pages. And keep the whole thing to one page. If you don't give an editor more than he/she can scan during a quick count of five, you just might have captured their attention.

Be professional. It's enough that any reviewer or editor for the book review section of a newspaper or magazine will already know that if they haven't heard of you before, odds are, you are a small press publisher. This doesn't mean they're biased against small presses. But many of these book reviewers receive a hundred times the amount of books they'll ever be able to review and the chances that they will read your book are already slim. Don't reduce your chances even more by sending out something that is poorly written.

Go back and look over all those query letters you wrote when you were trying to sell this thing to a publisher. Does it grab their interest? Does it bring the point home to its reader and make it personal to *them*? If so, you might want to dust it off, rework some of the terminology, and use it in your news release. You're still selling an idea – you still must be convincing – and you still want them to choose *your* book to read.

Don't limit the press releases to book review editors. If your book has a theme which, by its title, suggests something which a feature or even a news editor might be interested in it, send them one, too.

For instance, although my newest mystery, *ONLY ONE WAY OUT,* is considered fiction, much of the story is based on fact – names, dates, and actual events. It also addresses a critical current issue – illegal nuclear waste dumping. Which feature editors of the large East Coast newspapers received a copy? Or, at the least, a news release with a mail-back postcard on which they were invited to check off any book they wanted? Environmental editors, of course. Yes, I did find three or four of the larger newspapers which had them listed by name, and sent them a press release. And yes, I did hear from one and received an interesting mention in his column.

Many times, the book editor listed will actually assign your book to another reviewer. Don't worry about it. Remember, some of these papers get in hundreds of books a week – there's no way they can cover them all. Write a good news release, accompanied with a book review already written and ready for them to fill an empty space on a book-review page, and you just might have a chance. Sure, there'll be a lot of times your book will be reviewed and you won't even know it or if you do, you'll never get a copy of it. It doesn't matter. Your name and your book titles are getting out there – and that's what counts. The people who read that paper also shop in bookstores, as the people who own or manage those bookstores also read the newspapers.

Or you can always hire a clipping service. At the end of the following list of book reviewers are a few of their addresses.

• Follow Thru, Follow Thru, Follow Thru

I cannot stress enough just how important it is to *be persistent*. Give that book editor a call – ask him if he's on deadline, and if he's too busy to talk. If so, hang up and try again. If not, mention that you had mailed him a press release and that you're expecting this book to be a bestseller! And give him the reason why you feel this book will make it to the *New York Times* and *The Publisher's Weekly* bestsellers list. Your marketing plan.

I think you can do it, the same as I think I can. And why? *Because neither one of us will quit trying until it gets there!* Include in your envelope a mail-back postcard which can be made up at the local printers. A great money saver, as it will prevent you from sending out some 200 copies of the book – most of which would never have been read or reviewed. Those editors who truly want a sample copy are welcome to it and will actually fill in the card with their name and address and mail it back.

On one side, the card might look something like the text below – which is my own postcard. Try to imagine it on paper the size of a postcard. Put your book titles on the back with your return address on the front and a place to stick a stamp.

Yes, I'd like to have a review copy. Please send me the following;
( ) Only One Way Out
( ) Deadly Deceptions
( ) Hayseeds In My Hair
Company _____
Editor _____
Address _____
City, State _____

Below, you'll see the promised list of newspaper review editors. *Use it.* Copy it into your own mail-merge program, type it directly onto your word processor to be printed out onto blank sticky tapes, or directly onto your stationary, or simply write the addresses out by hand onto the envelopes. *Just use it.* It's yet another step in your successful writing/publishing effort.

Note: The rest of this book has hundreds of addresses, all of which will need to be typed into whatever program you'll be using. If you don't have a good set-up for that, try calling your local Community College or even your local Small Business Administration office, to see if they have a word processor you can use. Many of them will even have a program with classes to teach you how to use it. But, however you do it, and unless you plan to rent a mailing list, it's a good idea to start typing them *before* those books arrive. You'll be amazed at how time-consuming it can all be.

• Newspaper Book Review Editors

• ALABAMA •

Alabama Journal
200 Washington Avenue
PO Box 1000
Montgomery AL 36101-1000
205-262-1611
FAX: 205-261-1505
Jim Earnhardt, Book Editor

Birmingham News
2200 4th Avenue N
PO Box 2553
Birmingham AL 35202-2553
205-352-2466
FAX: 205-325-2283
Joey Kennedy, Book Reviewer

Birmingham Post Herald
2200 4th Avenue N
PO Box 2553
Birmingham AL 35202-2553
205-325-2222
FAX: 205-325-2410
Suzanne Dent, Book Editor

Huntsville Times
2317 Memorial Parkway S.
PO Box 1487
Huntsville AL 35807-1487
205-532-4000
Paige Oliver, Book Reviewer

Mobile Press-Register
304 Government Street
PO Box 2488
Mobile AL 36630-0002
205-433-1551
FAX: 205-434-8662
Gordon Tatum, Book Reviewer

Montgomery Advertiser-Journal
200 Washington Avenue
PO Box 1000
Montgomery AL 36101-1000
205-262-161
FAX: 205-261-1505
Jim Earnhardt, Book Editor

• ALASKA •

Anchorage Daily News
PO Box 149001
Anchorage AK 99514-9001
Thomas Harrison, Book Reviewer

Anchorage Times
820 West 4th Avenue
PO Box 100040
Anchorage AK 99501
907-279-5622
FAX: 907-263-9196
Ann Chandonnet, Book Editor

Juneau Empire
3100 Channel Drive
Juneau AK 99801
907-586-3740
Margaret Thomas,
    Book Reviewer

Homer News
3482 Landing Street
Homer AK 99603
907-235-7767
Jan O'Meara, Book Editor

• ARIZONA •

Arizona Daily Star
4850 S Park Ave., PO Box 26807
Tucson AZ 85726-6807
602-573-4132
FAX: 602-573-4144
J C Martin, Book Editor

Arizona Republic
120 E Van Buren., PO Box 1950
Phoenix AZ 85001-1950
602-271-8142
FAX: 602-271-8273
Tami Thornton, Book Editor

Phoenix Gazette
120 E Van Buren, PO Box 1950
Phoenix AZ 85001-1950
602-271-8900
FAX: 602-271-8911
Chris Lazelle, Book Editor

Tucson Citizen
4850 S Park Ave., PO Box 26767
Tucson AZ 85726-6767
Judy Carlock, Book Editor

Red Rock News
290 Van Buren, PO Box 619
Sedona AZ 86336
602-282-7795
FAX: 602-282-6011
Lois Stalvey, Book Reviewer

• ARKANSAS •

Arkansas Democrat-Gazette
Capitol Avenue and Scott Street
PO Box 2221
Little Rock AR 72203-2221
501-378-3400
FAX: 501-372-3908
Beth Soloman, Book Editor

Northwest Arkansas Times
PO Drawer D
Fayetteville AR 72702-1758
501-442-1777
FAX: 501-442-5477
Book Editor

• CALIFORNIA •

Alameda County/Bay Area
    Observer
PO Box 817
San Leandro CA 94577
510-483-7119

Alameda Times Star
4770 Willow
Pleasanton CA 94588
510-523-1205

Anaheim Bulletin
1771 S Lewis Street (92805-6498)
PO Box 7004
Anaheim CA 92825-0004
714-634-1567
FAX: 714-704-3748

Antelope Valley Press
PO Box 880
Palmdale CA 93590
805-273-2700
FAX: 805-947-4870

Antioch Ledger / Post Dispatch
1650 Cavallo Rd., PO Box 2299
Antioch CA 94531-2299
510-757-2525
Lisa Amand, Book Editor

Bakersfield Californian
1707 Eye St., PO Box 440
Bakersfield CA 93302-0440
Rick Heredia, Book Editor

The Californian
123 W Alisal St., PO Box 81091
Salinas CA 93912
408-424-2221
FAX: 408-754-4293
Tom Lee, Book Editor

Camarillo News
PO Box 385
Calistoga CA 94515
707-942-6242

Capistrano Valley News
23811 Via Fabricante
Mission Viejo CA 92691
714-768-3631

Chico Enterprise-Record
PO Box 9
Chico CA 95927
916-891-1234
Gary Kupp, Book Editor

Chico Enterprise-Record
c/o KFM Radio
PO Box 266
Chico CA 95927
919-343-8461
Dan Barnett, Book Reviewer

Contra Costa Times
PO Box 5088
Walnut Creek CA 94596-0088
510-935-2525
Carol Fowler, Book Editor

Daily Breeze
5215 Torrance Boulevard
Torrance CA 90509-4009
310-540-5511
FAX: 310-540-6272
Don Lechman, Book Editor

Daily Press
13891 Park Ave., PO Box 1389
Victorville CA 92393-0964
619-241-7744
FAX: 619-214-1860
Book Editor

Daily Variety
5700 Wilshire Boulevard # 120
Los Angeles CA 90036
213-857-6600
George Russell, Book Reviewer

29

Fairfield Daily Republic
1250 Texas St., PO Box 47
Fairfield CA 94533
707-425-4646
FAX: 707-425-5924
Ian Thompson, Book Staff
    Writer

Fremont Argus
3850 Decoto Road
Fremont CA 94536
510-794-0111
Barry Caine, Book Editor

Fresno Bee
1626 E Street
Fresno CA 93786-0001
Cathy Clarey, Book Editor

Glendale News-Press Leader
111 N Isabel St., PO Box 991
Glendale CA 91209-0991
818-241-4141
Book Editor

Grass Valley Union
PO Box 1025
Grass Valley, CA 95945
916-273-9561
Paul Harrar, Book Editor

Hayward Daily Review
116 W Winton Ave.
PO Box 5050
Hayward CA 94544
510-783-6111
Sharon Betz, Book Editor

Hollywood Reporter
5055 Wilshire 6th Floor
Hollywood CA 90036
213-525-2000
FAX: 213-525-2777
Attn: Book Editor

Imperial Valley Press
205 N 8th Street
El Centro CA 92244
619-352-2211
Don Quinn, Book Editor

Inland Valley Daily Bulletin
PO Box 4000
Ontario CA 91761
714-987-6397
Chris Reed, Book Editor

Long Beach Press Telegram
604 Pine Ave., PO Box 230
Long Beach CA 90844-0001
310-435-1161
FAX: 310-437-7892
Tim Grobaty, Book Editor

Los Angeles Daily News
PO Box 4200
Woodland Hills, CA 91365
818-713-3130
Kate Seago, Book Editor

Los Angeles Times Book Review
Times Mirror Square
Los Angeles CA 90053
213-237-5000
FAX: 213-237-7190
Sonja Bolle, Book Editor

Marin Independent Journal
PO Box 151790
San Rafael CA 94915
415-883-8600
Rebecca Larsen, Book Editor

Merced Sun Star
3033 North G St., PO Box 739
Merced CA 95341-0739
Book Editor

Modesto Bee
1325 H St., PO Box 3928
Modesto CA 95352-3928
209-578-2000
M A Mariner, Book Editor

Monterey Herald
Monterey Peninsula Herald Co
PO Box 271
Monterey CA 93942
408-372-3311
FAX: 408-372-8401
Dennis Sharp Book Editor

Napa Register
1615 Second St., PO Box 150
Napa CA 94559
707-226-3710
Book Editor

News Chronicle
2595 Thousand Oaks Boulevard
PO Box 3129
Thousand Oaks CA 91359
805-496-3211
FAX: 805-494-4523
Ray Hughey, Book Editor

Northeast Newspapers of LA
5420 N Figueroa Street
Los Angeles CA 90042
213-259-6225
Book Editor

The Oakland Tribune
66 Jack London Sq
Oakland CA 94607-3731
510-645-2000
FAX: 510-645-2771
Diane Ketchum, Book Editor

Oceanside Blade-Tribune
1722 S Hill, PO Box 90
Oceanside CA 92054-0018
619-433-7333
Debbie Rosen, Book Editor

Orange County Register
625 N Grand Ave.
PO Box 11626
Santa Ana CA 92701
David Whiting, Book Editor

Oxnard Press Courier
300 W Ninth Street
Oxnard CA 93030
805-483-1101
Book Editor

Palm Springs Desert Sun
750 N Gene Autry Trail
PO Box 2734
Palm Springs CA 92263-0190
Dick Kleiner, Book Reviewer

Petaluma Argus-Courier
830 Petaluma Boulevard N
PO Box 1091
Petaluma CA 94953
707-762-1707
FAX: 707-765-1707
Richard Bamner, Book Editor

Placerville Mountain Democrat
PO Box 1088
Placerville CA 95667
Book Editor
916-622-1255

Pleasanton Valley Times
126 Spring St., PO Box 607
Pleasanton CA 94566
510-462-4160
FAX: 510-847-2177

Redding Record-Searchlight
PO Box 492397
Redding CA 96049-2397
916-243-2424
Laura Christman, Book Editor

Riverside Press Enterprise
3512 14th St., PO Box 792
Riverside CA 92502-0792
714-684-1200
FAX: 714-782-7572
Joel Blain, Book Editor

Sacramento Bee
2100 Q St., PO Box 15779
Sacramento CA 95852
916-321-1000
FAX: 916-321-1109
Paul Craig, Book Editor

Sacamento Union
301 Capitol Mall., PO Box 2711
Sacramento CA 95812-2711
916-442-7811
FAX: 916-440-0524
Steve Connell, Book Editor

San Bernardino Sun
399 N D Street
San Bernardino CA 92401
714-889-9666
FAX: 714-885-8741
John Weeks, Book Editor

San Diego Daily Transcript
PO Box 85469
San Diego CA 92186
619-232-4381
FAX: 619-236-8126
Book Editor

San Diego Union/Tribune
350 Camino de la Reina
PO Box 191
San Diego CA 92112-4106
619-299-3131
FAX: 619-299-2333

San Francisco Chronicle
901 Mission Street
San Francisco CA 94103-2905
415-777-1111
FAX: 415-512-8196
Patricia Holt, Book Editor

San Francisco Examiner
110 Fifth St., PO Box 7260
San Francisco CA 94120
415-777-2424
FAX: 415-777-2525
Book Editor

San Gabriel Valley Daily Tribune
1210 Canyon Road (91790)
PO Box 1259
Covina CA 91722
818-962-8811
Brian Cochran, Book Editor

San Jose Mercury News
750 Ridder Park Drive
San Jose CA 95190
408-920-5000

San Mateo Times
1080 S Amphlett Boulevard
PO Box 5400
San Mateo CA 94402-0400
415-348-4321
FAX: 415-348-4446
Rick Eymer, Book Editor

Santa Barbara News Press
PO Box 1359
Santa Barbara CA 93102-1359
805-564-5200
FAX: 805-966-6258
Joan Crowder, Book Editor

Santa Cruz Sentinel
207 Church St., PO Box 638
Santa Cruz CA 95061-0638
408-423-4242
Christine Watson, Book Editor

Santa Maria Times
PO Box 400
Santa Maria CA 93456
805-925-2691
Sherry Wittman, Book Editor

Santa Monica Outlook
1920 Colorado Avenue (90404)
PO Box 590
Santa Monica CA 90406-0590
310-829-6811
Book Editor

Sonora Union Democrat
84 S Washington Street
Sonora CA 95370
209-532-7151
Kathe Waterbury, Book Editor

Stockton Record
530 E Market Street
PO Box 900
Stockton CA 95201-0900
Betty Liddick, Book Editor

Telegram Tribune
1321 Johnson, PO Box 112
San Luis Obispo CA 93406-0112
805-595-1111
FAX: 805-595-1211
Book Editor

Times-Advocate
207 E Pennsylvania Avenue
Escondido CA 92025
619-745-6611
FAX: 619-745-3769
Laura Grouch, Book Editor

Turlock Journal
138 S Center, PO Box 800
Turlock CA 95381
209-634-9141
Book Editor

Ukiah Daily Journal
590 S School St., PO Box 749
Ukiah CA 95482
707-468-0123
FAX: 707-468-5780
Book Editor

Ventura County Star-Free Press
5250 Ralston St., PO Box 6711
Ventura CA 93006
805-656-4111
FAX: 805-650-2944
Book Editor

Watsonville Register-Pajaronian
1000 Main S. PO Box 50055
Watsonville CA 95076-3732
408-724-0611
FAX: 408-722-8386
Candace Atkins, Book Editor

Whittier Daily News
PO Box 581
Whittier CA 90608
310-698-0955
Book Editor

Yuba-Sutter Appeal-Democrat
1530 Ellis Lake Drive
Maryville CA 95901
916-741-2345
FAX: 916-741-0140
Book Editor

Berkeley East Bay Express
PO Box 3198
Berkeley CA 94703
510-652-4610
Michael Covino, Book Reviewer

LA Weekly
PO Box 29905
Los Angeles CA 90027
213-667-2620
FAX: 213-667-2322
Kit Rachlis, Editor

Los Angeles Reader
5550 Wilshire Boulevard #301
Los Angeles CA 90036-3889
213-965-7430
Steven Kane, Book Editor

Palo Alto Weekly
703 High St., PO Box 1610
Palo Alto CA 94302-1610
415-326-8210
FAX: 415-326-3928
Don Kazak, Book Reviewer

Pasadena/Altadena Weekly
50 S Delacey Ave #200
Pasadena CA 911015
818-584-1500
Dan O'Heron, Book Editor

San Diego Reader
PO Box 85803
San Diego, CA 92186-5803
619-235-3000
Judith Moore, Book Reviewer

San Francisco Bay Guardian
520 Hampshire Street
San Francisco CA 94110-1417
415-255-3100
Book Editor

San Francisco Weekly
425 Brannan
San Francisco CA 94107
415-541-0700
Laura Miller, Book Editor

Santa Barbara Independent
607 State Street
Santa Barbara CA 93101
805-965-5205
FAX: 805-965-5518
Marianne Partridge, Editor

• COLORADO •

Denver Post
1560 Broadway, PO Box 1709
Denver CO 80201
303-820-1010
FAX: 303-820-1369
Glenn Giffin, Book Editor

Gazette Telegraph
30 S Prospect St., PO Box 1779
Colorado Springs CO 80901-
1779
719-632-5511
Linda DuVal, Book Editor

Grand Junction Daily Sentinel
734 S Seventh St., PO Box 668
Grand Junction CO   81501-7737
303-242-5050
Kathy Jordan, Book Editor

Pueblo Chieftain
825 West 6th St. PO Box 4040
Pueblo CO   81003
719-544-3520
Mary Porter, Book Editor

Rocky Mountain News
400 West Colfax Ave.
PO Box 719
Denver CO   80201
303-892-5000
FAX: 303-892-5499
Margie Carlin, Book Editor

• CONNECTICUT •

The Chronicle
Chronicle Road
Willimantic CT   06226
203-423-8466
FAX: 203-423-7641
Terese Karmel, Book Editor

Connecticut Post
410 State Street
Bridgeport CT   06604-4568
203-333-0161
FAX: 203-384-1158

Hartford Courant
285 Broad Street
Hartford CT   06115
203-241-6549
Jocelyn McClurg, Book Editor

Meriden Record-Journal
11 Crown S., PO Box 915
Meriden CT 06450
203-235-1661

Middletown Press
2 Main Street
Middletown CT   06457-3407
203-347-3331
FAX: 203-347-3380
Book Editor

New Haven Register
40 Sargent Drive
New Haven CT   06511
203-789-5200
Hayne Bayless, Book Editor

Stamford Advocate
75 Tresser Boulevard
Stamford CT   06904-3304
203-964-2200
FAX: 203-964-2345
Geoff O'Connell, Book Editor

Waterbury Republican American
389 Meadow S., PO Box 2090
Waterbury CT   06722-2090
203-574-3636
FAX: 203-596-9277
Jack Dailey, Book Editor

• DELAWARE •

Delaware State News
Webbs Lane & New Burton Road
PO Box 737
Dover DE   19903
302-674-3600
Gwen Guerke, Book Editor

The News Journal Company
PO Box 15505
Wilmington DE   19850-5505
302-324-2500
FAX: 302-324-5509
Charles Walker, Book Editor

• DISTRICT OF COLUMBIA •

Washington Post
1150 15th Street NW
Washington DC   20071-0001
202-334-6000
Linda Hales, Book Editor
Nina King, Book Editor
(send copy to each one)

Washington Times
3600 New York Avenue NE
Washington DC   20002
202-636-3000
FAX: 202-269-3419
Colin Walters, Book Reviewer

• FLORIDA •

Boca Raton News
33 SE Third Street
Boca Raton FL   33429
407-338-4920
FAX: 407-338-4944
Lona O'Connor, Book Editor

Bradenton Herald
102 Manatee Ave. W
PO Box 921
Bradenton FL   34206
813-748-0411
Book Editor

Florida Times Union
1 Riverside Ave., PO Box 1949-F
Jacksonville FL   32231
904-359-4111
FAX: 904-359-4478
Book Editor

Florida Today
1 Gannett Plaza
PO Box 419000
Melbourne FL   32940-9000
407-242-3500
FAX: 407-242-6620
Hanna Krause, Book Editor

Fort Lauderdale Sun-Sentinel
200 E Las Olas Boulevard
Fort Lauderdale FL   33301-2293
305-761-4000
FAX: 305-356-4676
Chauncey Mabe, Book Editor

Lakeland Ledger
Lime & Missouri Streets
PO Box 408
Lakeland FL   33802-0408
813-687-7000
Book Editor

Miami Herald
One Herald Plaza
Miami FL   33132-1609
305-350-2111
FAX: 305-376-3509
Margaria Fichtner, Book Editor

The News Journal
901 Sixth Street
PO Box 2831
Daytona Beach FL   32117-2831
904-252-1511
John Wirt, Book Editor

The News Press
2442 Dr Martin Luther King Blvd
PO Box 10
Fort Myers FL 33902-0010
813-335-0200
FAX: 813-335-0239
Drew Sterwald, Book Editor

Orlando Sentinel
633 N Orange Avenue
PO Box 2833
Orlando FL 32802-2833
407-420-5000
Nancy Pate, Book Editor

Palm Beach Post
2751 S Dixie Highway
West Palm Beach FL 33405
Tom Blackburn, Book Editor
407-820-4100

Pensacola News Journal
1 News Journal Plaza
PO Box 12710
Pensacola FL 32574-2710
904-435-8500
Book Editor

Sarasota Herald Tribune
PO Box 1719
Sarasota FL 34230
813-953-7755
FAX: 813-957-5276
Barbara Smith, Book Editor

St Petersburg Times
490 First Ave. S.,PO Box 1121
St Petersburg FL 33731
813-893-8111
FAX: 813-893-8675
Margo Hammond, Book Editor

Tallahassee Democrat
277 N Magnolia Dr., PO Box 990
Tallahassee FL 32302-0990
Book Editor

Tampa Tribune
202 S Parker St., PO Box 191
Tampa FL 33601
813-272-7600
FAX: 813-223-4316
Joe Guidry, Book Editor

The Tribune
600 Edwards Rd., PO Box 69
Fort Pierce FL 33482
305-461-2050
Book Editor

• GEORGIA •

Atlanta Journal & Constitution
72 Mariette Street NW
PO Box 4689
Atlanta GA 30302
404-526-5440
FAX: 404-526-5766
Don O'Briant, Book Editor

Augusta Chronicle & Herald
725 Broad St., PO Box 1928
Augusta GA 30903-1928
706-724-0851
Book Editor

Columbus Ledger & Enquirer
17 West 12th St., PO Box 711
Columbus GA 31994-1099
706-324-5526
Dusty Nix, Book Editor

Gainesville Times
PO Box 838
Gainesville GA 30503
404-532-1234
Book Editor

Gwinnett Daily News
200 Hampton Green
Duluth GA 30136
404-381-8535
Amy Blellew, Book Editor

Macon Telegraph & News
120 Broadway, PO Box 4167
Macon GA 31213-4199
912-744-4200
Paul Alexander, Book Editor

Marietta Daily Journal
580 Fairground Street
Marietta GA 30060-2797
404-428-9411
FAX: 404-422-9533
Book Editor

Savannah News-Press
111 W Bay Street
Savannah GA 31401-1191
912-236-9511
Larry Powell, Book Editor

• HAWAII •

Honolulu Advertiser
605 Kapiolani Blvd.
PO Box 3110
Honolulu HI 96802-3110
808-525-8090
FAX: 808-525-8037
Wanda Adams, Book Editor

Honolulu Star-Bulletin
605 Kapiolani Blvd.
PO Box 3080
Honolulu HI 96802
808-525-8640
FAX: 808-523-8509
Burl Burlingame, Book Editor

• IDAHO •

Idaho State Journal
305 S Arthur St., PO Box 431
Pocatello ID 83204-3306
208-232-4161
Book Editor

Idaho Statesman
1200 N Curtis Road
PO Box 40
Boise ID 83707-0040
208-377-6400
Book Editor

Lewistown Tribune
505 C St. PO Box 957
Lewiston ID 83501-1843
208-743-9411
John McCarthy, Book Editor

• ILLINOIS •

The Beacon News
101 South River Street
Aurora IL 60506
708-844-5844
Tom Johnson, Book Editor

Bloomington Pantagraph
301 W Washington Street
PO Box 2907
Bloomington IL 61702-2907
309-829-9411
Book Editor

Champaign News Gazette
15 Main St., PO Box 677
Champaign IL 61824-0677
217-351-5252
FAX: 217-351-5291
Tom Kacich, Book Editor

Chicago Sun-Times
401 N Wabash
Chicago IL 60611-3593
312-321-3000
FAX: 312-321-3084
Henry Kisor, Book Editor

Chicago Tribune
435 N Michigan Avenue #400
Chicago IL 60611-4022
312-222-3232
FAX: 312-222-3143
Diane Donovan, Book Editor

Daily Herald
217 W Campbell St., PO Box 280
Arlington Heights IL 60006-1411
708-870-3600
FAX: 708-398-0172
Cheryl terHortst, Book Editor

Daily Southtown Economist
5959 S Harlem
Chicago IL 60638-3187
312-586-8800
George Haas, Book Editor

Decatur Herald & Review
601 E Williams St. PO Box 311
Decatur IL 62525-1802
217-429-5151
Book Editor

Glesburg Register Mail
140 S Prairie Street
Galesburg IL 61401-4605
309-343-7181

Pantagraph
301 W Washington Street
Bloomington IL 61702
309-829-9411
Steve Gleason, Book Editor

Peoria Journal Star
1 News Plaza
Peoria IL 61643-0001
309-686-3000
Book Editor

Rockford Register-Star
99 E State Street
Rockford IL 61104
815-987-1200
Book Editor

State Journal-Register
1 Copley Plazza, PO Box 219
Springfield IL 62705
217-788-1303
FAX: 217-788-1551
Mike Kienzler, Book Editor

• INDIANA •

Bloomington Herald-Times
19000 S Walnut St., PO Box 909
Bloomington IN 47402-0909
812-332-4401
Book Editor

Columbus Republic
333 Second Street
Columbus IN 47201
812-372-7811
Book Editor

Evansville Courier
300 E Walnut Street
Evansville IN 47713-1938
812-424-7711
Book Editor

Fort Wayne Journal-Gazette
600 W Main St., PO Box 88
Fort Wayne IN 46801-0088
Pam Heinecke, Book Editor

Gary Post-Tribune
1065 Broadway
Gary IN 46402-2998
219-881-3000
Book Editor

Indianapolis News
307 Pennsylvania St.
PO Box 145
Indianapolis IN 46204-1811
L T Brown, Book Editor

Indianapolis Star
307 Pennsylvania St.
PO Box 145
Indianapolis IN 46206
317-633-1240
FAX: 317-633-9209
Richard Cady, Book Editor

Lafayette Journal & Courier
217 N Sixth Street
Lafayette IN 47901-1420
317-423-5511
John Fisher, Book Editor

Muncie Evening Press
125 S High St., PO Box 2408
Muncie IN 47302-0408
317-747-5700
Ellen Ball, Book Editor

Muncie Star
125 S High St., PO Box 2408
Muncie IN 47302-0408
317-747-5700
Rodney Ritchey, Book Editor

South Bend Tribune
225 W Colfax Avenue
South Bend IN 46626-0001
219-233-6161
Linda McManus, Book Editor

The Times
601 45th Street
Munster IN 46321
219-933-3200
FAX: 219-933-3249

• IOWA •

Cedar Rapids Gazette
500 Third Avenue SE
Cedar Rapids IA 52401-1619
319-398-8211
FAX: 319-398-5846
Bridget Janus, Book Editor

Des Moines Register
715 Locust St., PO Box 957
Des Moines IA 50304
515-284-8000
Joan Bunke, Book Editor

The Fairfield Ledger
112-114 East Broadway
PO Box 171
Fairfield IA 52556
515-472-4129

Iowa City Press-Citizen
1725 North Dodge.
PO Box 2480
Iowa City IA 52244
319-337-3181
Lynn Feuerbach, Book Reviewer

Ottumwa Courier
213 E Second Street
Ottumwa IA 52501-2902
515-684-4611
FAX: 515-684-7834

Quad City Times
500 East 3rd St., PO Box 3828
319-383-2314
FAX: 319-383-2370

Sioux City Journal
Sixth and Pavonia Streets
Sioux City IA 51102
712-279-5075
Bruce Miller, Book Reviewer

Waterloo Courier
501 Commercial Street (50701)
PO Box 540
Waterloo IA 50704
319-291-1400
FAX: 319-291-2060

• KANSAS •

Emporia Gazette
517 Merchant Street
Emporia KS 66801-4060
316-342-4800
Book Editor

Hutchinson News
PO Box 190
Hutchinson KS 67504-0190
316-662-3311
Jan Biles, Book Editor

Topeka Capitol-Journal
Stauffer Communications
616 Jefferson
Topeka KS 66607-1120
913-295-1111
FAX: 913-295-1230
Book Editor

Wichita Eagle
825 East Douglas St.
PO Box 820
Wichita KS 67201
316-268-6000
FAX: 316-268-6627
Chuck Potter, Book Editor

• KENTUCKY •

Frankfurt State Journal
321 W Main Street
Frankfurt KY 40601
502-227-4556
Book Editor

Kentucky New Era
PO Box 729
Hopkinsville KY 42240-4430
502-886-4444
David Jennings, Book Editor

Kentucky Post
421 Madison Avenue
Covington KY 41011-1519
606-292-2642
FAX: 606-291-2525
Book Editor

Lexington Herald-Leader
100 Midland Avenue
Lexington KY 40508-1712
606-231-3100
FAX: 606-254-9738
Paula Anderson, Book Editor

Louisville Courier-Journal
525 West Broadway
Louisville KY 40202-2206
502-582-4011
Keith Runyon, Book Editor

• LOUISIANA •

The Advocate
525 Lafayette St., PO Box 588
Baton Rouge LA 70821-0588
504-383-1111
Book Editor

Lake Charles American Press
4900 Hwy 90 East, PO Box 2893
Lake Charles LA 70602-2893
318-433-3000

The Monroe News-Star
411 N Fourth Street
Monroe LA 71201-6743
318-322-5161
FAX: 318-362-0225
Kelly McElroy, Book Editor

New Orleans Times-Picayune
3800 Howard Avenue
New Orleans, LA 70140-1097
504-826-3448
FAX: 504-826-3401
Susan Larson, Book Editor

Shreveport Times
222 Lake Street
Shreveport LA 71101-3738
318-459-3200
Lane Crockett, Book Editor

• MAINE •

Bangor Daily News
491 Main St., PO Box 1329
Bangor ME 04401-6243
207-990-8000
FAX: 207-941-9476

Lewiston Daily Sun
104 Park Street
Lewiston ME 04240-7202
207-784-5411
Lisa Giguere, Book Editor

Portland Press Herald
390 Congress St., PO Box 1460
Portland ME 04101-1103
207-780-9000
FAX: 207-780-9499
Jane Lord, Book Editor

• MARYLAND •

Baltimore Sun
501 N Calvert Street
Baltimore MD 21278-0001
410-332-6000
FAX: 410-332-6666
Timothy Warren, Book Editor

The Capitol
Capital-Gazette Newspapers
2000 Capitol Drive
Annapolis MD 21401
301-268-5000
Book Editor

• MASSACHUSETTS •

Berkshire Eagle
75 South Church Street
Pittsfield MA 01201
413-447-7311
Ruth Bass, Book Editor

Boston Globe
135 Morrissey Boulevard
PO Box 2378
Boston MA 02107-2378
617-929-2897
Gail Caldwell, Book Editor

Boston Herald
One Herald Square
PO Box 2096
Boston MA 02106
617-426-3000
FAX: 617-423-0887
Steve Morgan, Book Editor

Boston Phoenix
126 Brookline Avenue
Boston MA 02115
617-536-5390
David Barber, Book Reviewer

Brockton Enterprise
60 Main Street
PO Box 1450
Brockton MA 02403
617-586-6200
Fred Nobles, Book Editor

Cape Cod Times
319 Main Street
Hyannis MA 02601-4004
508-775-1200
FAX: 508-775-7337
North Cairn, Book Editor

Christian Science Monitor
1 Norway Street
Boston MA 02115-3195
617-450-2000
Cynthia Hanson, Book Editor

Daily Hampshire Gazette
115 Conz St., PO Box 299
Northampton MA 01060-3891
413-584-5000
FAX: 413-585-5222
Book Editor

Daily News
23 Liberty Street
Newburyport MA 01950
508-462-6666
Book Editor

Daily Times Chronicle
One Arrow Drive
Woburn MA 01801-2090
617-933-3700
FAX: 617-932-3321
James Hagerty III, Book Editor

Eagle Tribune
100 Turnpike St., PO Box 100
Lawrence MA 01842
508-685-1000
Book Editor

Fall River Herald-News
207 Pocasset Street
Fall River MA 02721-1599
617-676-8211
Tom Ward, Book Editor

Lowell Sun
15 Kearney Square
PO Box 1477
Lowell MA 01853-1477
Book Editor

Malden Evening News
38 Exchange Street
Lynn MA 01903
617-593-7700
Book Editor

Marlboro Enterprise/
 Hudson Daily
230 Maple Street
Marlboro MA 01752
508-485-5200
Barbara Courtemanche, Book
 Editor

Middlesex Daily News
33 New York Av., PO Box 800
Framingham MA 01701
508-626-3800
Pat Hyde, Book Editor

New Bedford Standard Times
555 Pleasant Street
New Bedford MA 02740-6235
508-997-7411
FAX: 508-997-7852
John Ackerman, Book Editor

Patriot Ledger
400 Crown Colony Drive
PO Box 498
Quincy MA 02169-0931
617-786-7000
Jon Lehman, Book Editor

Salem Evening News
155 Washington Street
Salem MA 01970
508-744-1010
FAX: 508-744-1010
Book Editor

Springfield Union News
The Republican Company
1860 Main Street
Springfield MA 01101
413-788-1264
FAX: 413-788-1301

Sun Chronicle
34 S Main S., PO Box 600
Attleboro MA 02703-2920
508-226-5851
FAX: 508-226-5851

The Transcript-Telegram
120 Whiting Farms Road
Holyoke MA 01040-2897
413-536-2300
FAX: 413-536-7414

Worcester Telegram & Gazette
20 Franklin Street
Worcester MA 01613
508-793-9100
FAX: 508-793-9281
Nicholas Basbane, Book Editor

• MICHIGAN •

Ann Arbor News
340 E Huron Street
Ann Arbor MI 48106-1909
313-994-6825
FAX: 313-994-6879
Anne Valentine, Book Editor

Battle Creek Enquirer
155 W Van Buren
Battle Creek MI 49017-3002
616-964-7161
Book Editor

Bay City Times
311 Fifth STreet
Bay City MI 48708-5853
517-895-8551
FAX: 517-895-5910
Wallace Town, Book Editor

Daily Tribune
210 E 3rd Street
Royal Oak MI 48067-2603
313-541-3000
Book Editor

Detroit Free Press
321 W Lafayette Boulevard
Detroit MI 48226
313-222-6400
FAX: 313-222-5981
Linnea Lannon, Book Editor

Detroit News
615 W Lafayette Boulevard
Detroit MI 48226
313-222-2300
FAX: 313-222-2335
Ruth Coughlin, Book Editor

Flint Journal
200 E First Street
Flint MI 48502-1925
313-767-0660
Gene Mierzejewski, Book Editor

Grand Rapids Press
155 Michigan Avenue NW
Grand Rapids MI 49503-2563
616-459-1400
Ann Byle, Book Editor

Kalamazoo Gazette
401 S Burdick St., PO Box 2007
Kalamazoo MI 49007
616-345-3511
Kathy Doud, Book Editor

Lansing State Journal
120 E Lenawee Street
Lansing MI 48919-0001
517-377-1000
Kathleen Iavey, Book Editor

Macomb Daily
67 Cass Avenue
Mount Clemens MI 48043-2347
313-469-4510
Mitch Kehetian, Book Editor

Oakland Press
48 W Huron, PO Box 9
Pontiac MI 48342
313-332-8181
FAX: 313-332-885
Book Editor

Port Huron Times Journal
911 Military Street
Port Huron MI 48061-5009
313-985-7171
FAX: 313-984-4230
Book Editor

Saginaw News
203 S Washington Avenue
Saginaw MI 48607-1283
517-752-7171
FAX: 517-752-3115
Penny Nickel, Book Editor

Detroit Monitor
33490 Groesbeck
Fraser MI 48026
313-296-6007
FAX: 313-296-6072
Horst Mann, Book Reviewer

• MINNESOTA •

Minneapolis Star Tribune
425 Portland Avenue South
Minneapolis MN 55488-0001
612-673-4000
FAX: 612-673-4359
Matthew Flann, Book Editor
Dave Wood, Book Editor

News-Tribune & Herald
424 W First Street
PO Box 169000
Duluth MN 55816-9000
218-723-5281
FAX: 218-723-5295
J P Furst, Book Editor

St Cloud Times
3000 North 7th Street
PO Box 768
St Cloud MN 56302
612-255-8700
FAX: 612-255-8704
Book Editor

St Paul Pioneer Press Dispatch
345 Cedar Street
Saint Paul MN 55101-1014
612-222-5011
FAX: 612-228-5500
Mary Ann Grossman, Book
    Editor

City Pages
401 N Third Street #550
PO Box 59183
Minneapolis MN 55459-0183
612-375-1025
Terri Sutton, Book Editor

Minnesota Women's Press
771 Raymond Avenue
Saint Paul MN 55114
612-646-3968
Mollie Hoben, Editor

Twin Cities Reader
5500 Wayzata Boulevard #800
Minneapolis MN 55418
612-591-2500
Glen Worchol, Editor

• **MISSISSIPPI** •

Clarion Ledger
311 E Pearl Street
Jackson MS 39205
601-961-7000
Jana John, Book Editor

Delta Democrat-Times
988 N Broadway
PO Box 1618
Greenville MS 38702
601-335-1155

McComb Enterprise-Journal
112 Oliver Emmrich Driver
McComb MS 39648-3903
601-684-2421
FAX: 601-684-0836
Book Editor

Natchez Democrat
503 N Canal Street
PO Box 1447
Natchez MS 39120
601-442-9101
Stacy Granig, Book Editor

• **MISSOURI** •

Columbia Missourian
PO Box 917
Columbia MO 65205
314-442-3161

Daily Quill
125 Jefferson
West Plains MO 65775-2774

Independence Examiner
410 S Liberty Street
Independence MO 64050-3850
816-254-8600
FAX: 816-836-3850
Audrey Stubbart, Book Editor

Jefferson City News & Tribune
210 Monroe Street
Jefferson City MO 65101-3210
314-636-3131
Fax: 314-636-7035
Dwight Warren, Book Editor

Joplin Globe
117 E Fourth Street
Joplin MO 64801
417-623-3480
FAX: 417-623-8450
Book Editor

Kansas City Star
1729 Grand Avenue
Kansas City MO 64108-1413
816-234-4141
Steve Paul, Book Editor

Springfield News-Leader
651 Boonville Avenue
Springfield MO 65806-1105
417-836-1100
Everett Kennell, Book Editor

St Joseph News Press
9th & Edmond Streets
PO Box 29
Saint Joseph MO 64502-0029
816-271-8500
Book Editor

St Louis Post-Dispatch
900 N Tucker Boulevard
Saint Louis MO 63101-1099
314-340-8000
Jim Creighton, Book Editor

The Riverfront Times
Hartmann Publishing
1221 Locust Street #900
Saint Louis MO 63103
314-231-6666
FAX: 314-231-9040
Saffir Ahmed, Book Editor

• MONTANA •

Billings Gazette
401 North Broadway
Billings MT 59101
406-657-1200
FAX: 406-657-1208
Christine Meyers, Book Reviewer

Bozeman Daily Chronicle
32 S Rouse St., PO Box 1188
Bozeman MT 59771
406-587-4491
FAX: 406-587-7995
Book Editor

The Missoulian
PO Box 8029
Missoula MT 59807
406-523-5240
FAX: 406-523-5221
Ginny Merriam, Book Editor

• NEBRASKA •

Lincoln Journal/Star
926 P St., PO Box 81609
Lincoln NE 68501
Herb Hyde, Book Editor

Omaha World Herald
World Herald Square
Omaha NE 68102
402-444-1000
FAX: 402-345-0183
Book Editor

• NEVADA •

Las Vegas Review-Journal
1111 W Bonanza Rd., PO Box 70
Las Vegas NV 89125-0070
702-385-4241
Book Editor

Las Vegas Sun
121 S Martin L King Boulevard
PO Box 4275
Las Vegas NV 89127
702-385-3111
FAX: 702-383-7264

Reno Gazette Journal
200 Bath St., PO Box 22000
Reno NV 89520-2000
Book Editor

• NEW HAMPSHIRE •

Claremont Times
Route 2
Claremont NH 03743-2504
603-542-5121
Bob Condon, Book Reviewer

Concord Monitor
1 Monitor Dr., PO Box 1177
Concord NH 03302
603-224-5301
Steve Varnum, Book Editor

The Union Leader
100 William Loeb Drive
PO Box 9555
Manchester NH 03108
603-668-4321
FAX: 603-668-0382
Barry Palmer, Book Reviewer

• NEW JERSEY •

Asbury Park Press
3601 Highway 66
PO Box 1550
Neptune NJ 07753
908-922-6000
FAX: 908-922-4818
Wally Stroby, Book Editor

Atlantic City Press
22 Devins Lane
Pleasantville NJ 08232
609-272-1100
Alice Post, Book Editor

Bridgewater Courier-News
1201 Route 22, PO Box 6600
Bridgewater NJ 08807-0600
908-722-8800
Book Editor

Camden Courier-Post
301 Cuthbert Blvd., PO Box 530
Cherry Hill NJ 08034
609-663-6000
Bill Reinhardt, Book Editor

Central New Jersey Home News
123 How Lane, PO Box 551
New Brunswick NJ 08903-0551
908-246-5500
FAX: 908-246-6046
Book Editor

Daily Record
629 Parsippany Road
Parsippany NJ 07054
201-428-6200
Cindy Smith, Book Editor

Jersey Journal
30 Journal Square
Jersey City NJ 07306-4199
201-653-1000
Book Editor

Newark Star Ledger
Star Ledger Plaza
Newark NJ 07101
201-877-4141
Roger Harris, Book Editor

The News Tribune
1 Hoover Way
Woodbridge NJ 07095-9990
908-442-0400
FAX: 908-442-1205
Charles Paolino, Book Editor

Passaic Herald News
988 Main Avenue
Passaic NJ 07055
201-365-3100
Michael Starr, Book Editor

The Record
Bergen Record Company
150 River Street
Hackensack NJ 07601-7110
201-646-4349
FAX: 201-646-4135
Book Editor

The Times
500 Perry Street
PO Box 847
Trenton, NJ 08605-0847
609-396-3232
FAX: 609-394-2819
Scotia Macrae, Book Editor

The Trentonian
600 Perry Street
Trenton NJ 08618-3996
609-989-7800
FAX: 609-393-6072
Book Editor

• NEW MEXICO •

Albuquerque Journal
7777 Jefferson Street NE
PO Drawer J
Albuquerque NM 87103
505-823-3912
FAX: 505-823-3994
David Steinberg, Book Editor

Albuquerque Tribune
PO Drawer T
Albuquerque NM 87103
505-823-3665
FAX: 505-823-3689
Kevin Hellyer, Book Editor

Roswell Daily Record
2301 N Main St., PO Box 1897
Roswell NM 88130
505-622-7710
FAX: 505-625-0421
Book Editor

Santa Fe New Mexican
202 E Marcy Street (87501)
PO Box 2048
Santa Fe NM 87504
505-983-3303
FAX: 505-986-9147
Book Editor

• NEW YORK •

Albany Times-Union
PO Box 15000
Albany NY 12212-5000
518-454-5420
Book Editor

Binghamton Press
Vestal Parway East
PO Box 1270
Binghamton NY 13902-1270
607-789-1234
Lou Brancaccio, Book Editor

Buffalo News
1 News Plaza
PO Box 100
Buffalo NY 14240-0100
716-849-4444
FAX: 716-856-5150
Jeff Simon, Book Editor

Evening Observer
8-10 East Second Street
Dunkirk NY 14048
716-366-3000
Ted Lutz, Book Editor

Ganette Suburban Newspapers
One Gannett Drive
White Plains NY 10604-3406
914-694-9300
FAX: 914-694-5018
Pamela Cristine, Book Editor

New York Daily News
220 West 42nd Street
New York NY 10017
212-210-2100
FAX: 212-661-4675
Sherryl Connelly, Book Editor

New York Newsday
2 Park Avenue
New York NY 10016
212-251-6850
FAX: 212-696-0487
Jennifer Krauss, Book Editor

New York Post
210 South Street
New York NY 10002-7807
212-815-8000
FAX: 212-815-8470
Matthew Slamm, Book Editor

New York Times Book Review
229 West 43rd Street
New York NY 10036-3959
Rebecca Sinkler, Book Editor

Newsday
235 Pinelawn Road
Melville NY 11747-4250
516-454-2020
Book Editor

Poughkeepsie Journal
85 Civic Center Plaza
PO Box 1231
Poughkeepsie NY 12602-1231
914-454-2000
FAX: 914-437-4921
Tony DeBarrows, Book Editor

Rochester Democrat-Chronicle
55 Exchange Boulevard
Rochester NY 14614-2001
716-232-7100
Michael Johansson, Book Editor

Rochester Times Union
55 Exchange Street
Rochester NY 14614-2001
716-232-7100
Bob Palmer, Book Editor

Schenectady Gazette
2345 Maxon Road
Schenectady NY 12308
518-374-4141
Sherryl McGill, Book Editor

Staten Island Advance
950 Fingerboard Road
Staten Island NY 10305-1495
718-981-1234
FAX: 718-981-5679
Mark Hanley, Book Editor

Syracuse Herald-Journal
Clinton Square
PO Box 4915
Syracuse NY 13221-4915
315-470-2265
FAX: 315-470-3019

Syracuse Post Standard
PO Box 4818
Syracuse NY 13221-4818
315-470-0011
FAX: 315-470-3081
Jim McKeever, Book Editor

Times Herald-Record
40 Mulberry Street
Middletown NY 10940-6302
914-343-2181
FAX: 914-343-2170
Moe Mitterling, Book Editor

Wall Street Journal
200 Liberty Street
New York NY 10281-0001
212-416-2500
FAX: 212-416-3299

Watertown Daily Times
260 Washington Street
Watertown NY 13601-3364
315-782-1000
FAX: 315-782-2337
Book Editor

Brooklyn Paper Publications
26 Court Street
Brooklyn NY 11242-0104
Book Editor

Phoenix Newspaper
395 Atlantic Avenue
Brooklyn NY 11217-1797
Michael Armstrong, Book Editor

Queens Tribune
174-15 Horace Harding
Expressway
Fresh Meadows NY 11365
718-357-7400
Book Editor

The Village Voice
36 Cooper Square
New York, NY 10003-4846
212-475-3300
FAX: 212-475-8944
M Mark, Book Reviewer

• **NORTH CAROLINA** •

Asheville Citizen-Times
14 O'Henry Ave., PO Box 2090
Asheville NC 28802-8594
704-252-5611
FAX: 704-251-2659
Dale Neal, Book Editor

Charlotte Observer
600 S Tryon St., PO Box 32188
Charlotte NC 28232-6094
704-358-5000
Dannye Romaine, Book Editor

Durham Hearld Sun
2828 Picket St., PO Box 2092
Durham NC 27702-2092
919-419-6900
Ed Hodges, Book Editor

Fayetteville Observer & Times
458 Whitfield Rd., PO Box 849
Fayetteville NC 28302
919-323-4848

Greensboro News & Record
200 E Market Street
Greensboro NC 27420
919-373-7001
FAX: 919-373-7067
Ann Morris, Book Editor

High Point Enterprize
210 Church Avenue
PO Box 1009
High Point NC 27261
919-888-3500   919-841-5582

Raleigh News Observer
215 S McDowell Street
Raleigh NC 27602
919-829-4500
Michael Skube, Book Editor

Rocky Mount Evening Telegram
150 Howard St., PO Box 1080
Rocky Mount NC 27802
919-446-5161
Mae Bell, Book Editor

Salisbury Post
PO Box 4639
Salisbury NC 28144-0105

Winston-Salem Journal
418 N Marshall Street
PO Box 3159
Winston-Salem NC 27101-2815
919-727-7394
FAX: 919-727-7315
Linda C Brinson, Book Editor

• NORTH DAKOTA •

Grand Fords Herald
120 N Fourth Street
PO Box 6008
Grand Forks ND 58206
701-780-1114
FAX: 701-780-1123
Marcia Harris, Book Editor

• OHIO •

Akron Beacon Journal
44 E Exchange Street
PO Box 640
Akron OH 44309
216-996-3000
FAX: 216-996-3075
Joan Rice, Book Review Editor

Canton Repository
500 Market Avenue S
Canton OH 44702-2195
216-454-5611
Gary Brown, Book Reviewer

Cincinnati Enquirer
312 Elm Street
Cincinnati OH 45201
513-721-2700
FAX: 513-768-8340
Ann Hicks, Book Editor

Cincinnati Post
125 East Court Street
Cincinnati OH 45202
513-352-2785
FAX: 513-621-3962
Maureen Conian, Book Editor

Cleveland Plain Dealer
1801 Superior Avenue NE
Cleveland OH 44114-2107
216-344-4500
FAX: 216-344-4809
Janice Harayda, Book Editor

Columbus Dispatch
34 S Third Street
Columbus OH 43215-4241
614-461-5000
George Myers Jr, Book Editor

Dayton Daily News
45 S Ludlow St., PO Box 1287
Dayton OH 45402
513-225-2000
Bety Dietz-Krebs, Book Editor

Elyria Chronicle Telegram
PO Box 4010
Elyria OH 44036
216-329-7000
FAX: 216-329-7154
Jack Morgan, Book Editor

Lake County News Herald
38879 Mentor Road
Willoughby OH 44094
216-951-0000
FAX: 216-951-0917
Patricia Ambrose, Book Editor

Toledo Blade
541 N Superior Street
Toledo OH 43660-0001
419-245-6000
FAX: 419-245-6439

Vindicator
Vindicator Square
PO Box 780
Youngstown OH 44501-0780
216-747-1471
FAX: 216-747-6712
Mike Braun, Book Editor

• OKLAHOMA •

Ada Evening News
116 N Broadway
Ada OK 74820-5004
405-332-4433

Chickasha Daily Express
302 N 3rd
Chickasha OK 73018
405-224-2600

Oklahoman
25 NW 4th, PO Box 25125
Oklahoma City OK 73125-0125
405-475-3331
Ann De Frange, Book Editor

Tulsa World
318 South Main Mall
PO Box 1770
Tulsa OK 74102-1770

• OREGON •

Eugene Register Guard
975 High Street
PO Box 10188
Eugene OR 97440-2188
503-485-1234

Medford Mail Tribune
33 N First St., PO Box 1108
Medford OR 97501
503-776-4411
Bill Varble, Book Editor

The Oregonian
1320 SW Broadway
Portland OR 97201-3469
503-221-8327
FAX: 503-227-5306
Paul Pintarich, Book Editor

Salem Statesman-Journal
280 Church Street NE
PO Box 13009
Salem OR 97309-1015
503-399-6611
FAX: 503-399-6808
Grant Butler, Book Editor

Willamette Week
2 NW Second Avenue
Portland OR 97209
Doug Halm, Book Reviewer

• PENNSYLVANIA •

Allentown Morning Call
101 N 6th Street
PO Box 1260
Allentown PA 18105-1260
215-820-6626
FAX: 215-820-6693
Paul Willistein, Book Editor

Beaver County Times
PO Box 400
Beaver PA 15009-0400
412-775-3200
Marsha Keefer, Book Editor

Bucks County Courier Times
8400 Route 13
Levittown PA 19057
215-752-6701
Milt Krugman, Book Editor

Daily Local News
250 N Bradford Avenue
West Chester PA 19382
215-696-1775
Book Editor

Erie Times-News
205 West 12th Street
Erie PA 16534-0001
814-870-1600
FAX: 814-870-1632
Ed Wellejus, Book Editor

The Express-Times
PO Box 391
Easton PA 18044-0391
215-258-7171
Book Editor

Greensburg Tribune-Review
Cabin Hill Drive
Greensburg PA 15601
412-838-5151
FAX: 412-838-5171
Book Editor

Harrisburg Patriot-News
812 Market St., PO Box 2265
Harrisburg PA 17105-2265
Nance Woodward, Book Editor

Johnstown Tribune Democrat
425 Locust St., PO Box 340
Johnstown PA 15907-0340
Ruth Rice, Book Editor

Lancaster New Era
8 West King Street
Lancaster PA 17603-3809
Book Editor

Philadelphia Daily News
400 N Broad St., PO Box 7788
Philadelphia PA 19101
215-854-5900

Philadelphia Inquirer
400 N Broad St., PO Box 8263
Philadelphia PA 19101
215-854-2000
FAX: 215-854-4794
Mike Leary, Book Editor

Pittsburgh Green Sheet
404 North Avenue
Pittsburgh PA 15209-2334
412-821-4012
FAX: 412-821-4012
Book Editor

Pittsburgh Post Gazette
50 Boulevard of the Allies
PO Box 566
Pittsburgh PA 15230
412-263-1601
FAX: 412-391-8452
Bob Hoover, Book Editor

Pittsburgh Press
34 Boulevard of the Allies
PO Box 566
Pittsburgh PA 15230-0566
412-263-1100
Sylvia Sachs, Book Editor

Reading Eagle Times
PO Box 582
Reading PA 19603-0582
215-371-5000
Karen Miller, Book Editor

The Scranton Times-Tribune
PO Box 3311
Scranton PA 18505
717-348-9100
Michelle Solomon, Book Editor

York Dispatch/York Sunday News
205 N George
York PA 17401-1124
717-854-1575
FAX: 717-843-2958
Pam Saylor, Book Editor

German Town Paper
2923 W Scheltanham
Philadelphia PA 19150
215-885-4111

Philadelphia Northeast Times
8033 Frankford Avenue
Philadelphia PA 19136-2736
John Scanlan, Editor

The Post
Montgomery Publishing
PO Box 61310
Fort Washington PA 19034
215-337-1700
FAX: 215-337-9850
Patti Schmidt, Editor

• RHODE ISLAND •

Providence Journal-Bulletin
75 Fountain Street
Providence RI 02902-7000
Carol McCabe, Book Editor

• SOUTH CAROLINA •

Anderson Independent-Mail
Po Box 2507
Anderson SC 29622
803-224-4321

Charleston Post & Courier
134 Columbus Street
Charleston SC 29403-4809
803-577-7111
Margaret Garrett, Book Editor

Columbia State
1401 Shop Rd., PO Box 1333
Columbia SC 29202
803-771-8374
William W Starr, Book Editor

The Greenville News
305 S Main St., PO Box 1688
Greenville SC 29602
803-298-4110
FAX: 803-298-4395

Spartanburg Herald-Journal
189 Main Street
Spartanburg SC 29306
803-582-4511
Scott Kearns, Editor

Sun News
914 Frontage Rd E (29577)
PO Box 406
Myrtle Beach SC 29578
803-448-8352
FAX: 803-626-0356

• SOUTH DAKOTA •

Argus Leader
200 S Minnesota, PO Box 5034
Sioux Falls SD 57117
605-331-2200
Ann Grauvogl, Book Editor

Pierre Capitol Journal
333 W Dakota
Pierre SD 57501
605-224-7301
Leta Nolan, Book Editor

• TENNESSEE •

Chattanooga News-Free Press
400 East 11th Street
Chattanooga TN 37402
615-756-6900
FAX: 615-757-6383
Karen Glendenning, Book Editor

Chattanooga Times
117 E Tenth St., PO Box 951
Chattanooga TN 37401
615-756-1234
FAX: 615-267-4036
Wes Hasden, Book Editor

The Commercial Appeal
495 Union Avenue
Memphis TN 38103-3242
901-529-2211
FAX: 901-529-2522
Fred Koeppel, Book Editor

Jackson Sun
PO Box 1059
Jackson TN 38301-6126
901-427-3333
Jaque Hillman, Book Editor

Johnson City Press-Chronicle
204 West Main Street (37601)
PO Box 1717
Johnson City TN 37605-1717
Brad Jolly, Book Editor

Kingsport Times-News
701 Lynn Garden Drive
PO Box 479
Kingsport TN 37662-5607
615-246-8121
FAX: 615-392-1392
Book Editor

Knoxville News-Sentinel
208 W Church
PO Box 59038
Knoxville TN 37950-9038
Jan Avent, Book Editor

Maryville Daily Times
PO Box 9740
Maryville TN 37802-9740
615-981-1100
FAX: 615-981-1175
Book Editor

Nashville Banner
1100 Broadway
Nashville TN 37203-3116
615-259-8800
FAX: 615-259-8890
Sue McClure, Book Editor

Nashville Tennessean
1100 Broadway
Nashville TN 37203-3116
Robert Wyatt, Book Editor

• TEXAS •

Abilene Reporter-News
101 Cypress St., PO Box 30
Abilene TX 79604-0030
Larry Lawrence, Book Editor

Amarillo Globe-News
900 Harrison, PO Box 2091
Amarillo TX 79166
806-376-4488
FAX: 806-376-9217
Mary Kate Tripp, Book Editor

Austin American-Statesman
305 S Congress, PO Box 670
Austin TX 78764
512-445-3500
FAX: 512-445-3679
Steve Levin, Book Editor

Beaumont Enterprise
380 Main, PO Box 3071
Beaumont TX 77701-2359
409-838-2803
FAX: 409-838-2857
Book Editor

Corpus Christi Caller-Times
820 Lower Broadway
PO Box 9136
Corpus Christi TX 78469-9136
Book Editor

Dallas Morning News
PO Box 655237
Dallas TX 75365-5237
214-977-8222
Robert Compton, Book Editor

El Paso Herald-Post
300 North Campbell, PO Box 20
El Paso TX 79901-1426
915-546-6100
Charles Edgren, Book Editor

Fort Worth Star-Telegram
400 W 7th St., PO Box 1870
Fort Worth TX 76101
817-390-7400
FAX: 817-390-7789
Larry Swindell, Book Editor

Houston Chronicle
801 Texas Ave., PO Box 4260
Houston TX 77210
713-220-7171
George Christian, Book Editor

Houston Post
4747 SW Freeway
PO Box 4747
Houston TX 77210-4747
Elizabeth Bennett, Book Editor

Lubbock Avalanche-Journal
PO Box 491
Lubbock TX 79408-0491
806-762-8844
William E Kerns, Book Editor

Lufkin Daily News
PO Box 1089
Lufkin TX 75902-1089
409-632-6631
Jay Milner, Book Editor

Pasadena Citizen
PO Box 6192
Pasadena TX 77506-0192
713-477-0221
FAX: 713-477-9090
Clay Zeigler, Book Editor

San Angelo Standard-Times
PO Box 5111
San Angelo TX 76902-5111
915-653-1221
Diane Murray, Book Editor

San Antonio Express News
Avenue E and 3rd Street
PO Box 2171
San Antonio TX 78297-2171
512-225-7411
Judith Rigler, Book Editor

San Antonio Light
420 Broadway, PO Box 161
San Antonio TX 78205
512-271-2700
Steve Bennet, Book Editor

Texarkana Gazette
315 Pine Street
Texarkana TX 75501-5683
903-794-3311
FAX: 903-792-7183
William Blackman, Book Editor

Times Record-News
1301 Lamar, PO Box 120
Wichita Falls TX 76307-0120
817-767-8341
FAX: 817-767-5201
Louise Gregg, Book Editor

Tyler Courier-Times Telegraph
410 W Erwin St., PO Box 2030
Tyler TX 75702-7188
Everett Taylor, Book Editor

Waco Tribune Herald
900 Franklin Ave., PO Box 2588
Waco TX 76702-1100
817-757-5757
FAX: 817-757-0302
Carl Hoover, Book Editor

• UTAH •

Deseret News
30 East 100 South
PO Box 1257
Salt Lake City UT 84110
801-237-2100
Jerry Johnston, Book Editor

Ogden Standard-Examiner
455 23rd St., PO Box 951
Ogden UT 84402-0951
801-394-7711
Vanessa Zimmer, Book Editor

Salt Lake Tribune
143 S Main St., PO Box 867
Salt Lake City UT 84110-0867
801-237-2011
Harold Schindler, Book Editor

• **VERMONT** •

Barre Times-Argus
540 N Main Street
Barre VT 05641-2504
802-479-0191
Ann Gibbons, Editor

Burlington Free Press
191 College St., PO Box 10
Burlington VT 05402-0010
802-863-3441
FAX: 802-862-5622
Molly Walsch, Book Editor

Rutland Daily Herald
27 Wales Street
Norwich VT 05701
802-775-5511
Lee Huntington, Book Critic

• **VIRGINIA** •

Daily Press
7505 Warwick Blvd.
PO Box 746
Newport News VA 23607-0746
804-247-4600
Will Molineux, Book Editor

Richmond Times Dispatch
PO Box 85333
Richmond VA 23293
804-649-6000
Ann L Merriman, Book Editor

Roanoke Times & World-News
201 Campbell Avenue SW
PO Box 2491
Roanoke VA 24010-1105
703-981-3100
Mike Mayo, Book Editor

USA Today
1000 Wilson Boulevard
Arlington VA 22229
703-276-3400
Robert Wilson, Book Editor

Virginian Pilot/Ledger-Star
150 W Brambleton Avenue
Norfolk VA 23510-2018
804-446-2000
FAX: 804-446-2414
Ann Sorjesma, Book Editor

• **WASHINGTON** •

Bremerton Sun
545 5th St., PO Box 259
Bremerton WA 98310-1413

Everett Herald
Grand & California Avenues
PO Box 930
Everett WA 98206-0930
206-339-3000
Diane Wright, Book Editor

Morning News Tribune
1950 S State St., PO Box 11000
Tacoma WA 98411
206-597-8649
FAX: 206-597-8274
Don Ruiz, Book Editor

The Olympian
1268 4th Ave. E, PO Box 407
Olympia WA 98507-4212
206-754-5400

Seattle Post-Intelligencer
101 Elliot Avenue W
Seattle WA 98119-4220
206-448-8000
FAX: 206-448-8166
M L Lyke, Book Reviewer

Seattle Times
PO Box 70
Seattle WA 98111
206-464-2111
FAX: 206-464-2261
Donn Fry, Book Editor

Spokesman-Review
999 W Riverside
PO Box 2160
Spokane WA 99201
509-459-5413
FAX: 509-459-5482
Dan Webster, Book Editor

Vancouver Columbian
PO Box 180
Vancouver WA 98666-0180
Brian Cantrell, Book Editor

Walla Walla Union-Bulletin
PO Box 1358
Walla Walla WA 99362
509-525-3300
Book Editor

Yakima Herald-Republic
114 N 4th St., PO Box 9668
Yakima WA 98909
509-248-1251
Book Editor

The Seattle Weekly
Sasquatch Publishing Co
1931 Second Avenue
Seattle WA 98101-1199
206-441-6238
FAX: 206-441-6213

Northwest Parent Publishing
2107 Elliott Avenue # 303
Seattle WA 98121
206-565-4004
FAX: 206-441-6213
Ann Bergman, Editor

West Seattle Herald
3500 SW Alaska Street
Seattle WA 98126-2731
206-932-0300
Shauna Brown, Editor

• WEST VIRGINIA •

Charleston Daily Mail
1001 Virginia Street E
Charleston WV 25301-2816
304-348-4870
FAX: 304-348-4847
Becky Fleming, Book Reviewer

Herald-Dispatch
946 Fifth Avenue
Huntington WV 25701-2004
304-526-4000
FAX: 304-522-3138
James McMiller, Book Reviewer

Wheeling News Register
1500 Main Street
Wheeling WV 26003
304-233-0100
Book Editor

• WISCONSIN •

Appleton Post Cresent
306 W Washington St.
PO Box 59
Appleton WI 54912
414-733-4411
Maureen Blaney, Book Editor

Green Bay Press-Gazette
435 E Walnut, PO Box 19430
Green Bay WI 54307-9430
414-435-4411
Warren Gerds, Book Reviewer

Milwaukee Journal
333 W State St., PO Box 661
Milwaukee WI 53201-0661
414-224-2000
FAX: 414-224-2047
Roger K Miller, Book Editor

Milwaukee Sentinel
918 N 4th St., PO Box 371
Milwaukee WI 53203-1506
414-224-2151
FAX: 414-224-2049
Ernie Franzen, Book Editor

Wisconsin State Journal
1901 Fish Hatchery Rd.
PO Box 8058
Madison WI 53708-8058
608-252-6100
FAX: 608-252-6333
Brian Howell, Book Editor

• WYOMING •

Casper Star Tribune
PO Box 80
Casper WY 82602
307-266-0500
Wyoma Groenenberg, Book
  Editor

Wyoming Eagle
702 W Lincolnway
Cheyenne WY 82001
307-634-3361
FAX: 307-778-7163
Book Editor

Wyoming State Tribune
702 W Lincolnway
Cheyenne WY 82001
307-634-3361
FAX: 307-778-7163
Book Editor

· CHAPTER FIVE ·

SEND THOSE BABIES OUT AND DON'T BE STINGY

*Congratulations! Your books have been delivered. They're gorgeous – and ready to sit on a bookstore shelf. You are now a published author **and** a publisher. It's a great book and it's time to tell the world. But to do that, you've got to get them ordering from you.*

· Galleys

Some magazine editors will want galleys *only*. That's because of the timing and scheduling. They need time to read the book, write the review, and to get it onto the magazine page before or at about the same time the book will be available to the general public. They will have nothing to do with a book once it has been printed. See that they get a galley – even if you have to take your one and only set of bluelines and run copies off yourself on a copy machine.

I have made notations on the following list, of those particular editors who accept *galleys only*.

These are the things that pay off. Some other editors will accept an early review copy but you must get it to them hot off the presses!

· Magazine Book Review Editors

Publisher's Weekly
PW Forecasts
249 West 17th Street
New York, NY 10011
(Galleys only)
Book Review Editors;
Sybil Steinberg, fiction
Genevieve Stuttaford, nonfiction
    hardcovers
Penny Kaganoff, paperbacks

Diane Roback, children's books
Molly McQuade, how-to-books

Kirkus Reviews
200 Park Avenue South #1118
New York, NY 10003-1543
(Galleys only)
Ann Larsen, fiction
Jeffrey Zaleski, nonfiction
Joanna Long, children's books

• Booklist •

American Library Association
50 E Huron Street
Chicago, IL 60611
(312) 944-6780
FAX (312) 440-0901
John Mort, adult books
Sally Estes, young adult books
Ilene Cooper, children's books
Sandy Whiteley, reference books
Write for a copy of the *Procedures for Submitting Review Materials* at the above address.

Library Journal
249 West 17th Street
New York, NY 10011
(212) 463-6816
FAX (212) 242-6987
Barbara Hoffert, Managing
Editor, Book Review Section

School Library Journal
249 West 17th Street
New York, NY 10011
(212) 463-6757
FAX 212-442-6987
Trevelyn Jones, Book Review
Editor

Horn Book Magazine
14 Beacon Street
Boston, MA 02108
(617) 227-1555
FAX 617-523-0299
(Galleys only)
Anita Silvey, Editor

Choice
100 Riverview Center
Middletown, CT 06457;
(203) 347-6933
FAX 203-346-8586
(Galleys only)
Book Review Editor

New York Times Book Review
229 West 43rd Street
New York, NY 10036
(212) 556-1234
Rebecca Sinkler, Editor of Book
Review
Eden Ross Lipson, Children's
Book Editor
Christopher Lehmann-Haupt
Book Review for daily New York
Times

Washington Post Book World
1150 15th Street N.W.
Washington D.C. 20071
(202) 334-6000
FAX (202) 334-4480
Nina King, Editor

San Francisco Chronicle Book
Review
275 Fifth Street
San Francisco, CA 94103
(415) 777-7042
Patricia Holt, Book Review
Editor

Los Angeles Times Book Review
Times Mirror Square
Los Angeles, CA 90053
(212) 237-7000
FAX (213) 237-4712
Sonya Bolle, Book Review Editor

New York Newsday
2 Park Avenue
New York, NY 10016
(212) 251-6850
FAX (212) 696-0487
Jack Schwartz, Book Review
   Editor

Chicago Tribune Books
435 N Michigan Avenue
Room 400
Chicago, IL 66011-4022
(312) 222-3232
FAX (312) 222-3143
Diane Donovan, Book Review
   Editor

USA Today
1000 Wilson Boulevard
Arlington, VA 22209
(703) 276-3400
Robert Wilson, Book Editor

New York Review of Books
250 West 57th Street #1321
New York, NY 10107-0169;
(212) 757-8070
FAX (212) 333-5374
Robert B. Silvers or Barbara
   Epstein, Editors

San Francisco Review of Books
555 De Haro Street #220
San Francisco, CA 94107
(415) 252-7708
FAX (415) 252-8908
Jennifer Martinez, Managing
   Editor

Voice Literary Supplement
842 Broadway
New York, NY 10003
(212) 460-1477
Ms. M Mark, Editor

The Bloomsbury Review
1028 Bannock Street
Denver, CO 80204
(303) 892-0620
FAX (303) 892-5620
(Galleys only)
Tom Auer, Editor-in-Chief

Small Press Magazine
Moyer-Bell, Kymbolde Way
Wakefield, RI 02879
(401) 789-0074
FAX (401) 789-3793

Small Press Book Review
PO Box 176
Southport CT 06590
(203) 268-4878
Henry Berry, Editor

Small Press Review, Dustbooks
PO Box 100
Paradise CA 95969
(916) 877-6110
FAX (916) 877-0222
Len Fulton, Editor

• Specialty Magazines

Don't forget to focus on the specialty magazines. Almost any kind of book you might write has a corresponding magazine which is known to have an interest in that type of book. My books were mainly mysteries, so naturally the first copies to scoot out of here were to the *Alfred Hitchcock Magazine*, the *Armchair Detective*, and *Mystery Readers Journal*. In addition to that, since the themes surrounding many of my story-lines are centercd around the danger of losing forever our forests and bays to pollution, I also looked for newspaper editors who specialize in environmental columns. Listed below are a sampling of magazine book review editors. I highly suggest that you look for more. *The Book Publishing Resource Guide* by Marie Kiefer is an excellent place to start. Whether your books are regional history, a collection of poems, or your version of the great American novel, you'd do yourself credit by researching those magazines that seem to have the same interests as yours.

ABBWA Journal
David Lamb, Book Editor
PO Box 10548
Marina del Rey CA 90295
Focus: American Black Book
    Writers Journal
Reviews books of interest to
    blacks.

African Review
Joe Weixlmann, Editor
Department of English
Indiana State University
Terre Haute IN 47809
Focus: Minority reviews

Air Force Magazine
Frank Oliveri, Book Editor
Air Force Association
1501 Lee Highway
Arlington VA 22209-1198
Focus: General interest; non-
    fiction only.

Alaska Quarterly Review
Ronald Spatz, Editor
Department of English, U of AK
3211 Providence Drive
Anchorage AK 99508
Focus: Literary short story, poetry

Alfred Hitchcock Magazine
Mary Cannon, Book Reviewer
380 Lexington Avenue
New York, NY 10168-0035
Focus: Mysteries

Allure
Karen Marta, Book Editor
Conde Nast Publications
350 Madison Avenue
New York, NY 10017
Focus: Women's magazine

American Baby
Judith Nolte, Editor
Cahners Publishing
475 Park Avenue South
New York, NY 10016-6999
Focus: child development,
    parenting.

American Book Review
Don Laig, Editor
Publications Ctr., English Dept.
Box 494, University of Colorado
Boulder CO 80309
Focus: Art, fiction, poetry,
    general interest.

American Forests
Wallace Kaufman, Book
    Reviewer
1516 P St. NW., PO Box 2000
Washington DC 20013
Focus: Ecology, consevation,
    environmental issues.

American Girl
Harriet Brown, Book Editor
The Pleasant Company
8400 Fairway Place
Middleton WI 53562
Focus: Girls ages 7-12

American Heritage
Jane Colihan, Book Editor
60 Fifth Avenue
New York, NY 10011
Focus: History related, regional

American Literature
Cathy N Davidson, Editor
Duke University
304 E Allen Building
Durham NC 27706
Focus: Scholarly and critical
    books on American literature
    and culture.

American Poetry Review
Stephen Berg, Book Editor
1721 Walnut ST.
Philadelphia PA 19103
Focus: Poetry

American Scholar
Sandra Costich, Editor
1811 Q St NW
Washington DC 20009
Focus: Literary novels, literature,
    poetry, education.

American Voice Magazine
Frederick Smock, Editor
Broadway & 4th #1215
Louisville KY 40202
Focus: Poetry, literature, general
    fiction

Analog
Tom Easton, Book Reviewer
Stanley Schmidt, Editor
The Reference Library
380 Lexington Avenue
New York, NY 10168-0001
Focus: Science fiction, fantasy

The Antioch Review
Po Box 148
Yellow Springs OH 45387
Gary Bower, Book Reviewer
Jon Saari, Book Reviewer
David St. John, Poetry Editor
Focus: Literature, novels, general
    fiction, poetry,

Armchair Detective
Kathy Daniel, Editor
Mysterious Press
129 West 56th St
New York, NY 10019-3808
Focus: Mysteries

Army Magazine
Catherine O'Keffe, Editor
2425 Wilson Boulevard
Arlington VA 22201-3326
Focus: Non-fiction only - military,
    politics, nautical, aviation

The Atlantic Monthly
745 Boylston St.
Boston MA 02116
Phoebe-Lou Adams, Books Editor
Peter Davison, Poetry Editor
Focus: Fiction, poetry, general
   interest

Belles Lettres
Jane Bakerman, Reviewer
Mystery Books
RR 23, Box 131
Terre Haute IN 47802
Focus: Mysteries

Belles Lettres
Janet Mullaney, Editor
11151 Captain's Walk Court
Gaithersburg MD 20878
Focus: Literature by women

Belles Lettres
Michelle Tokarczyk, Reviewer
Poetry Books
130 West 16th St #61
New York, NY 10011
Focus: Poetry by women

Better World Magazine
David Alan Ramsdale, Book
   Reviewer
17211 Orozco
Granada Hills CA 91344
Focus: Health, environment, New
   Age, social issues

The Bloomsbury Review
1028 Bannock St.
Denver CO 80204
Tom Auer, Editor
(Galleys only)
Focus: Small press, general
   interest

The Book Reader
Jay Bail, Editor
245 Mt Hermon Road
Scotts Valley CA 95066
Focus: General interest, New
   Age, reviews
distributed to bookstores

BookLover
Editor
Reading Rage Publishing
151 West 75th St
New York, NY 10023-1844
Focus: General interest

Boston Review
Ms Kim Cooper, Editor
33 Harrison Avenue
Boston MA 02111
Focus: Arts, entertainment,
   literature, general fiction,
   poetry

Chattahoochee Review
Book Reviews
2101 Womack
Dunwoody GA 30338-4435
Focus: Fiction, poetry

The Circle
Ruth Denny, Editor
Minneapolis American Indian
   Center
1530 E Franklin Avenue
Minneapolis MN 55404
Focus: Native American interests

Columba; Midwest Review of
   Books
Jeanne Bonham, Co-Editor
101 E Wilson Bridge Road
Worthington OH 43085-2303
Focus: Fiction, mysteries,
   children's books

The Cookbook Review
Lise Stern, Editor
60 Kinnard St
Cambridge MA 02139
Focus: Cooking, food

Cooking Light
Katherine Eakin, Editor
2100 Lakeshore Dr
Birmingham AL 35209
Focus: Cooking, food, nutrition

Country Home
Beverly Hawkins, Editor
Meredith Corporation
1716 Locust St
Des Moines IA 50309-3023
Focus: General interest, book
excerpts and reviews

Current Books Magazine
Edwin Grosvenor, Editor
Washington Media Group
PO Box 34468
Bethesda MD 20827
Focus: General interest

Different Worlds
Editor
2814 19th St
San Francisco CA 94110
Focus: Science fiction, fantasy,
suspense, adventure novels

The Drood Review
Editor
PO Box 8872
Boston MA 02114
(Galleys only)
Focus: Mysteries

Earth First Journal
Time Bechtel, Co-Editor
PO Box 5176
Missoula MT 59806
Focus: Environment

Fessenden Review
Walter Brock, Editor
PO Box 7272
San Diego CA 92107-0272
Focus: Small press reviews,
general interest

Fiction
Editor
Heldref Publications
1319 Eighteenth St NW
Washington DC 20036-1802
Focus: Fiction

Gentlemen's Quarterly
Mordecai Richler, Book Editor
Books & Things
350 Madison Avenue
New York, NY 10017
Focus: General interest, upscale
men's magazine

Hudson Review
Paula Dietz, Co-Editor
Fredrick Morgan, Co-Editor
684 Park Avenue
New York, NY 10021-5043
Focus: General fiction, literary
novels, poetry

Iris: A Journal about Women
Rebecca Hyman, Editor
Corner Building 323 HSC
University of Virginia
Charlottesville VA 22908
Focus: Books by and for women

Military Magazine
Mike Mark, Editor/Book
  Reviewer
2122 28th St
Sacramento CA 95818
Focus: Military history, wars

Mirabella Magazine
Particia Towers, Book Editor
200 Madison Avenue
New York, NY 10016
Focus: General interest

Northwest Review
John Witte, Editor
369 PLC
University of Oregon
Eugene OR 97403
Focus: Literature, poetry

People Weekly
Kristin McMurran, Editor
Time-Life Building
1271 Avenue of the Americas
New York, NY 10020-1303
Focus: General interest, acquires
  & edits book excerpts

Ploughshares
DeWitt Henry
Emerson College
100 Beacon St
Boston MA 02116
Focus: Literature, poetry, literary
  novels, general interest

Poetry
Joseph Parisi, Editor
60 West Walton St
Chicago IL 60610
Focus: Poetry

Portland Review
Kala Rounds, Editor
Portland State University
PO Box 751
Portland OR 97207
Focus: Literature, poetry, literary
  novels, general fiction

USA Weekend
Marcia Bullard, Editor
1000 Wilson Blvd
Arlington VA 22229-0012
Focus: General interest

The Village Voice
Sarah Jewler, Editor
36 Cooper Square
New York NY 10003
Focus: General interest

Virginia Quarterly Review
Staige Blackford, Editor
One West Range
Charlottesville VA 22903
Focus: Literature, literary novels,
  fiction

Washington Review
Clarissa Wittenberg, Editor
PO Box 50132
Washington DC 20091
Focus: Arts, fiction, poetry

Women's Review of Books
Linda Gardiner, Editor
Center for Research on Women
Wellesley College
Wellesley MA 02181-8255
Focus: Women's issues

Science Fiction Age
Scott Edelman, Editor
487 Carlisle Drive
PO Box 749
Herndon VA 22070
Focus: Science Fiction

Science Fiction Chronicle
Don D'Ammassa, Book Editor
323 Dodge St.
East Providence RI 02914-4265

• Book Fairs, Trade Shows and Conventions

This is your chance to meet those bookstores owners and managers. Shake their hands, show them a copy of your book – even give them one if they're really interested. This is that magic moment when they are actively looking for books to carry on their shelves. They're not busy with customers and your conversation will not be interrupted every five minutes with their daily business of running a bookstore. They're shopping for books. And as each one of them stroll by your table, you'll have the opportunity to make your pitch. Now is when you show them the book. Let them hold it, read the title, thumb through the pages, and find out which distributors are carrying it. Be sure to give them a handful of your bookmarks, your business card, and a brochure if you have one.

It is also your chance to meet the distributors – especially if you've already contacted them and they have not returned the favor. Be sure to have your press kit handy. Keep it updated with the accomplishments you've already made and have it ready to show to the buyers at any moment. Include a mini-copy of your marketing plan. Not the details, such as budgeting or addresses, but an overall look at what your plans are. You'll want to give each buyer their own copy, but carrying all these things around all weekend can be a drag. After they've gotten a good gander at your books and the press kit, and you feel reasonably assured they'll remember your name, offer to mail the whole package to their home office.

You'll also have a chance to see what the other publishers have out there in the marketplace. Don't be shy. Ask lots of questions. Find out who's doing what and how it's working for them. What type of books are popular this season? What do they plan for next year? What's their favorite way of marketing?

Most of these conventions have excellent speakers – both informative and entertaining. These speakers are almost always authors. Learn from them: how the speaker views their books, their careers, and the book industry itself.

I have yet to come away from any one of these conferences and not be glad I went. The ideas, the networking, and the first-hand on-the-job training on how to enter this new, exciting world of publishing could never be learned in a better environment. If you can't go yourself, try to sign up with one of the co-ops so that your book will at least be seen.

• Free Advertising

In addition to reviews and articles, join everything you can imagine and get listed in their journals, reference books, magazines, trade show publications, and small press publications. On the following pages is a partial list of a number of organizations that can only help you learn more about the business you're entering and how to get the word out that you have a book worth looking at. *A Book Publishing Resource Guide* has a much more extensive list.

Note: Don't forget those conventions which might be interested in offering a seminar or workshop on the same subject as your book. Especially if you've written a 'how-to' book. Every special interest group has their own convention and whoever is in charge of lining up their agenda is probably looking for a new face and a new approach. In other words, someone just like you. And since you literally "wrote the book" on this particular subject, you're the expert. Research those conventions in your library and write them a proposal. If they don't want your workshop, let them know you are available to sit on a panel. You'll not only sell a ton of books, but you can use the money from those sales as a spring-board to launch your marketing plan. Besides the networking, it looks great on your profile and it may possibly get you a spot on a local radio or T.V. show.

ABA Convention
Eileen Dengle, Director
American Booksellers Assn.
560 White Plains Road
Tarrytown NY 10591
914-631-7800
FAX: 914-631-8391
Focus: Largest American trade
    show for booksellers
Dates: Early June

ALA Convention
Barbara Macikas, Director
American Library Association
50 East Huron Street
Chicago IL   60611
312-280-3219
FAX: 312-280-3224
Focus: Major library convention
Dates: July

International Festival of Author
International Readings Dept
Harbourfront Corporation
410 Queens Quay West
Toronto M5V 2Z3 ON Canada
416-973-4600
Dates: October

Miami Book Fair International
Dr Yillion Castro Coppolechia
Miami Dade Community College
300 NE Second Avenue # 1502
Miami FL 33132-2204
305-237-3258
FAX: 305-237-3645
Focus: General interest
Dates: November

Poetry Publication Showcase
Lee Briccetti, Director
Poets House
72 Spring Street 2nd Floor
New York NY 10012
212-431-7920
Focus: Poetry
Dates: Early June

SF Bay Area Book Festival
Elizabeth Whipple, Director
1095 Market Street # 402
San Francisco CA 94103
415-861-2665
FAX: 415-626-4317
Focus: General interest
Dates: October

Small Press Book Fair
Karin Taylor, Director
Small Press Center
20 West 44th Street
New York NY 10036
212-764-7021
Dates: Early December

For more information, contact the Director and ask for a sample copy of their literature and to be put on their mailing list.

EventLine
Po Box 57101
Philadelphia PA 19111
215-572-742
FAX: 215-572-7393
Focus: Trade shows and conventions

Exhibits Directory
Assn of American Publishers
220 East 23rd Street
New York NY 10010
212-689-8920
FAX: 212-696-0131
Focus: Trade shows

Sources of Information about
    Trade Shows and Expositions
Trade Show Bureau
1660 Lincoln Street #2080
Denver CO 80264
303-860-7626
FAX: 303-860-7479

• Co-Ops

If you cannot attend each and every one of the trade shows you'd like to, as very few of us can, try some of the co-ops. They will exhibit your book for you, along with all the other books whose publisher has signed up for the service, for a fee. They may not promote your book as well as you would, but it is exposure to the booksellers and librarians - which is better than nothing. Drop them a card and ask for a sample copy of their literature. Again, this is but a partial list.

Baker & Taylor Exhibit Service
Baker & Taylor
6 Kirby Avenue
Somerville NJ 08876
202-526-8000
Focus: International exhibits

COSMEP Exhibit Service
Richard Morris
PO Box 703
San Francisco CA 94101-0703
415-921-6190
Focus: Small press

New American Writing
Sarah Stonich
311 Ramsey Street
Saint Paul MN 55102
612-228-0577
Focus: Small press titles to
        Frankfurt

PMA Display Service
Jan Nathan
Publishers Marketing Association
2401 Pacific Coast Hwy # 102
Hermosa Beach CA 90254
310-372-2732
FAX: 310-374-3342
Focus: Co-op exhibits at book
        shows and conferences

• Publishing Associations

These can be invaluable for up-to-date information, giving you free listings in their publications and reference manuals, and access to some priceless networking. The following is a sample listing – you'll want to find those specialty associations which most closely associate with your work.

Academy of American Poets
Henri Cole, Director
Poetry Pilot Newsletter
177 East 87th Street
New York NY 10128
212-427-5665
Focus: Poetry writers

The Authors Guild
Peggy Randall, Asst Director
Authors Guild Bulletin
234 W 44th Street
New York NY 10036
212-398-0838
Focus: Writers

74

International Women's Writing
Guild
Hannelore Hahn, Director
Gracie Station
PO Box 810
New York NY 10028-0013
212-737-7536
Focus: Women writers and
publishers

The National Writers Club
Sandra Whelchel, Director
NWC Newsletter
1450 S Havana # 620
Aurora CO 80012
303-751-7844
FAX: 303-751-8593
Focus: Writers

National Writers Union
Kim Fellner, Director
American Writer Magazine
13 Astor Place Seventh Floor
New York NY 10003
212-254-0279
Focus: Writers

Pacific NW Writers Conference
Director
17345 Sylvester Road SW
Seattle WA 98166
206-242-9757
Focus: NW Writers

PEN American Center
Pamela Pearce
568 Broadway
New York NY 10012-3225
212-334-1660
Focus: Fiction, poetry writers

Poetry Society of America
Cynthia Atkins, Asst Director
15 Gramercy Park S
New York NY 10003
212-254-9628
Focus: Poetry writers

Poets & Writers
Elliot Figman, Director
Poets & Writers Magazine
72 Spring Street
New York NY 10012
212-226-3586
FAX: 212-226-3963
Focus: Poetry, fiction writers

Small Press Writers & Artists
Audre Parente
SPWAO Newsletter
328 Timberline Trail
Ormand Beach FL 32174
904-672-3085
Focus: Small press writers

Willamette Writers
Director
9045 SW Barbur Blvd # 5-A
Portland OR 97219
503-452-1592

• Booksellers Associations

Join as many of the booksellers associations as you can. It will be one of the best steps you have ever taken if you truly are committed to promoting that book of yours. As I mentioned before, the free advertising you'll get by inclusion in their newsletters each time you publish a new book or win a prize (or anything else you feel is worth crowing about) is absolutely priceless. In addition, many of them publish an annual catalog, and you'll get another free listing in that. The bookstores and libraries depend on these publications to let them know what's out there and to give them ideas on what to order.

Believe me, these are the professionals in the field of publishing. Watch them, read what they write, and listen carefully. You will learn more from these organizations than you can ever imagine.

American Booksellers Assn.
560 White Plains Road
Tarrytown, NY 10591
800-637-0037

Pacific Northwest Booksellers
    Association
1510 Mill St.
Eugene, OR 97401-4258

Book Publishers Northwest
PO Box 99642
Seattle, WA 98199
206-885-3173

Oregon Independent Booksellers
    Association
PO Box 230543
Tigard, OR 97281-0543
503-224-5097

• CHAPTER 6 •

WHOLESALERS AND DISTRIBUTORS

"How many a human has dated a new era in his life from the reading of a book."

— *Henry David Thoreau*

• Persistence Pays

Although all of the companies have their own way of doing business, there are basically two main differences between distributors and wholesalers: how they promote your book and how they pay.

For various reasons, some of which only they find reasonable, bookstores will seldom order directly from a publisher. They prefer ordering through their regular channels as with the distributor and/or a wholesaler. Therefore, it is essential that you connect with one or more of these distributor/wholesalers and have them stock your books in their warehouse.

This is not the easiest part of the marketing. Sometimes, they can be hard to work with, especially since a small, first-time publisher usually means more paperwork than profits for them. They may or may not answer your letters and your messages on their voice-mail machines seem to vanish into the ether. It's up to you to prove yourself to be "up to snuff" and worthy of the warehouse space.

But read on. There are ways ... and there are ways. With a great deal of perseverance, you will get their attention and a big, fat order.

Note: Usually, a smaller and more local distributor – such as one who distributes mostly to your state and a few bordering states – will have a small-press office set up especially for the local publishers and self-publishers. For instance, *Pacific Pipeline, (8030 South 228th Street, Kent, WA, 98032-2900, phone: (206) 872-5523)*, will almost always carry the books of a local publisher. They also have a sales rep who will take your book, along with all the others, and present them to the wholesalers such as *Waldenbooks, Barnes & Noble, Baker & Taylor and B.Dalton.* This is good news because their presentation will be much more effective than yours. The wholesalers will then order directly from *Pacific Pipeline.*

This does not mean you can sit back and rest on your laurels. To really get your books out there on a national level, you'll still need those larger, national distributors to give YOU a order and list it on their microfiche. If they've been contacted already by *Pacific Pipeline*, that's great. Contact them again. And again. This is where you'll use that great-looking stationary and your updated press kit. Send each of the distributor and wholesalers a package which includes the kit with a cover letter inside asking them to stock your book, a brief copy of your marketing plan that includes the approximate dates you intend to follow through with each phase of it (excluding the addresses of course), and a copy of the book. Be sure to mention the number of press releases you intend to send and to whom (such as 200 of the top book-review newspapers in the country, and 100 of the largest independent bookstores, and all of the major chain-store headquarters).

Once each of these companies has had time to receive your package, give them a call. If you don't know who the buyer is for your area, call the distributor/wholesaler and ask information for his/her name and extension. You may have to re-dial, but be sure to speak directly to that person and ask if they have received your press-kit and if they intend to place an order.

You may possibly be put off the first time you contact this buyer. Remember, this is not necessarily a '*no*'; it is a '*not right now.*' Then, each time you mail a news or press release, a mail-out of brochures, or any other promotional campaign, send this buyer one too. Eventually, he/she will be convinced that you mean business and will return your efforts with an order.

One thing you will want to remember is that these companies are not your enemies. They are made up of hard-working people just like yourself, trying to keep their jobs, trying to stay afloat. All they need to know is that you are a professional and that you intend to see this thing through to the end. That you won't be more of a hassle than you're worth, but will indeed make them some money. This, my friends, is called capitalism.

A rule of thumb for some of the distributors is that they'll look to see if you have at least four books in print. One way to satisfy that need is to form an organization with a group of friends who are also self-publishing. Put four viable and definitely saleable books together under one company name and you've just overcome another hurdle.

• If You Create The Demand, They Will Buy

It's up to you to create the demand for your books.

The different distributor/wholesaler companies all have different policies about promoting and marketing books. Some of them are quite active in the field, using all sorts of sales tools including catalogs and newsletters and telemarketing, not to mention the sales reps who call on the bookstores in person. All for a price. Some of the others do very little marketing on their own and operate basically as order-takers.

It's only natural that a reader who has seen your book reviewed in a newspaper or magazine, will check at their local bookstore to see if they carry it. They'll want to look at the book, read a page or two, before they decide to buy it. If they don't see it on the shelf, hopefully they'll ask about it at the counter.

The bookstore personnel will then begin to look through their lists of distributor/wholesalers to see who carries it. If none do – trust me on this – *they* will then be the ones to call their distributors and ask them to order it from the publisher (yourself). And orders for one or two books at a time will begin to trickle in.

Now, this doesn't sound like much in the beginning. But after 8 or 10 of these calls, somewhere in the darker depths of a distributor's warehouse, a light will come on. Bingo! You've got their attention. If they haven't sent you an order in the past, they'll probably use the *R.R. Bowker, Books In Print* to find your address, set up an account in your company name, and you'll suddenly receive a phone call asking for a direct and substantial order of your books.

Also, send your brochure to the entire membership of the *American Booksellers Association* – either from a mailing list or from their directory. Remember all those addresses you typed into your word processor? Those are bookstores that are actively shopping for books. Again – if your book is of the type they like to carry, they will hound those distributors for you.

'What'dya mean, you don't have that book? Who does have it?' Suddenly, your order is on its way. *PRONTO*.

Note: Whether they ask you or not, they're going to need to know up-front what your company policy is on returns. To save time and to help convince them they should place an order, have your policies typed up and include it in the press-kit when you first contact them. It's important that you agree to a *fully- returnable* contract, which means that they have the option of returning all unsold books at their discretion.

Once one of the larger distributors has agreed to take you on as a vendor, be sure to ask exactly what their policies are and how much will they participate in the marketing of your book. Don't forget to ask to see a copy of their catalog and a rate sheet for buying ad space in it and any other promotional publications.

Another excellent way to get some immediate sales going AND to attract the attention of the distributors is to sell directly to the buying public. The readers. This is why you need that brochure or postcard. Send your brochure directly to them. I've included, on the following pages, some of the companies who supply select mailing lists.

Many of these readers don't mind ordering a book by mail, directly from the publisher, especially if in the brochure has an order blank and you've promised to have the book autographed by the author. Be sure to have a State Revenue tax number by then so that you can collect sales tax. By the way – there's no middle-man, here. You'll be paid the entire amount of the retail price of your book plus shipping costs.

In your brochure, you'll want to provide them with an 800 number and credit-card-buying privileges. If you don't have these services available, try a "fulfillment service." In addition to the many services they provide, these companies will warehouse your books, provide an 800 number for you to use on your promotional material – answered 24 hours a day – and accept VISA or Mastercard charge orders over the phone. And if that's not enough, they pack and ship that order the same day.

To name only two:

Twin Peaks Press	BookMasters
PO Box 129	638 Jefferson St., Po Box 159
Vancouver, Washington 98666-0129	Ashland, Ohio, 44805
(206) 694-2462	(419) 289-6051

There are many others.

The down-side of working with distributors is that they are terribly late in paying you. It will be at least 90 days and up to four months before you'll get a check. And, if they've taken your books on consignment, that long-awaited payment will be for only the amount of books actually sold in that period. They'll return the rest, some of which have been fairly dog-eared. Expect this to happen and don't be disappointed or enraged. We all have to wait the same amount of time.

They will also expect a liberal policy for credits on returns. In other words, your books will be warehoused for just so long without any ongoing sales. After about three months with nothing happening, they will insist on having the prerogative to send them back to you with no prior notice. You'll also get back the books the stores have returned to them that haven't sold by the end of the season. The major chain stores are even faster about cleaning their shelves of any book that's not moving. Be sure to find out what kind of discount they will want from you. Most of the larger companies take 55%.

The upside to working with these companies is that they offer an incredibly valuable service for you, as you'd find the bookstore and the library market outside of your local area almost impenetrable without them. Be sure to find out if this is a company that offers sales representatives.

It's a good idea to include the sales reps in your mailings. If they hear from you often enough, they're guaranteed to get curious. Even if they sell only on commission, the exposure will be priceless. Your local booksellers associations, such as the *Pacific Northwest Booksellers Association (PNBA)* or the *American Booksellers Association (ABA)*, will have an up-to-date listing in their membership directory of those who operate in your area. I have not included it here, as the list changes each season and it would be out of date by the time this book goes to press. Also, the trade shows, put on by these booksellers associations, are an excellent place to meet these reps. If you know you're going to see them at the trade show, set up an appointment with a few of these reps in advance to show them your book and your marketing plan over lunch or coffee.

• Distributors

Contact each one of the distributors below, by looking for those who specialize in your type of book or carry all types (General interest). Send them a copy of the book and of your marketing plan. Then *be persistent*. Carry through with each facet of your own plan. Get your momentum going. If they have to catch up with you later on, that's fine. Don't worry about it. But don't slow down, either.

Book Publishing Resource Guide, by Marie Kiefer, has a much better selection of the companies who specialize.

Advent Books
C Kumble, President
141 East 44th Street
New York NY 10017-4006
212-697-0887
Subjects: Literature, world
history, social issues
Territory: International

Chicago Review Press
814 N Franklin Avenue
Chicago IL 60610
312-337-0747
FAX: 312-337-5985
800-888-4741
Subjects: General interest
Territory: US
Markets: Jobbers, bookstores,
libraries

Independent Publishers Marketing
Donna Montgomery, Buyer
6824 Oaklawn Avenue
Edina MN 55435
612-920-9044 800-669-9044
Subjects: Business, biographies,
    cookbooks, parenting, sports,
    general interest
Territory: US

International Circulation
Richard Dooda, Sales Director
Book Distribution
250 West 55th Street
New York NY 10019
212-649-4478
Subjects: General interest
Territory: US-CN
Markets: Jobbers, mass markets,
    bookstores, retail outlets

International Specialized Books
Jeannette Bokma, Buyer
5602 NE Hassalo Street
Portland OR 97213-3640
503-287-3093
FAX: 503-284-8859
800-547-7734
Subjects: Architecture, business,
    cookbooks, home, languages,
    travel, general
Territory: US-CN-IT (Cen/S
    Amer)
Markets: All markets

Library Book Selection Service
Larry Efaw, Manager
2714 McGraw Drive
PO Box 277
Bloomington IL 61704-0277
309-663-1411
FAX: 309-664-0059
Subjects: Children's interests,
    young adult novels
Territory: US
Markets: Libraries

Login Publishers Consortium
Dominique Raccah or Mitch
    Rogatz
1436 W Randolph St 2nd Floor
Chicago IL 60607
312-733-8228
FAX: 312-666-2680
Subjects: Business, reference,
    general interest
Territory: US
Markets: Bookstores, libraries

National Book Network
Jed Lyons, President
4720 Boston WAy # A
Lanham MD 20706-4310
301-459-8696
FAX: 301-459-2118
800-462-6420
Subjects: Business, cookbooks,
    entertainment, history,
    politics, self-help, regional,
    travel
Territory: US-IN
Markets: Bookstores, jobbers

Paul & Company
Robert Paul, Owner
PO Box 442
Concord MA 01742
508-369-3049
FAX: 508-369-2385
Subjects: General interest
Territory: US-CN
Markets: Bookstores, libraries

Pendar Book Company
S R Akbarian, President
10471 S Amarylis
PO Box 6385
Salt Lake City UT 84106
801-572-2009
Territory: US
Markets: Bookstores

Publishers Distribution Corp
Bud McSweeney, Nat'l Cir Dir
PO Box 4371
Los Angeles CA 90078-4371
213-871-1225
FAX: 213-467-6805
Subjects: Automobiles, computers, gay/lesbian titles
Territory: US
Markets: Jobbers, newsstands

Publishers Distribution Service
Jerrold Jenkins, President
6893 Sullivan Road
Grawn MI 49637
Subjects: General interest
Territory: US-CN-IT
Markets: Bookstores, libraries, retail outlets

Publishers Group West
Karla Simmons, Acquisitions Editor
4065 Hollis St., PO Box 8843
Emeryville CA 94662
510-658-3453
FAX: 510-658-1834
800-788-3123
Subjects: Computer, children's books, business, family, health, travel, general interest
Territory: US
Markets: Bookstores, schools, libraries

Quality Books Inc
Amy Mascillino, Product Development
918 Sherwood Drive
Lake Bluff IL 60044-2204
708-295-2010
FAX: 708-295-1556
Subjects: General interest (nonfiction only)
Territory: US
Markets: Libraries

Spring Arbor Distributors
Phyllis Hedges, Adult Trade Buyer
Robert Stone, Bible Buyer
Susan Heuser, Children's Books
Tom Feia, Book Buyer, Religious Books
10805 Textile Road
Belleville MI 48111-2398
313-481-0900 800-521-3080
FAX: 313-483-9560
Subjects: Religious, General interest, children's
Territory: US-CN-IT
Markets: Bookstores, mass markets, religious stores

Unique Books
Richard Capps, Product Manager
4230 Grove Avenue
Gurnee IL 60031
708-623-9171 800-553-5446
FAX: 708-623-7238
Subjects: General non-fiction,
  children's books
Territory: US
Markets: US

• INTERNATIONAL
  DISTRIBUTORS •

Airlift Book Company
Don Skirving or Beth Grossman
26/28 Eden Grove
London NC8EL England
071-607-5792
FAX: 071-607-6714
Subjects: Women's interest,
  general interest (small press
  titles)
Territory: England
Markets: Bookstores, public
  libraries, jobbers

Birkhauser Verlag AG
Frank van Eck, Marketing
  Director
Ringstrasse 39
CH 4106 Therwil
Basil Switzerlnd
061-73-53-00
FAX: 061-73-14-27
Subjects: General interest
Territory: IT (Europe)
Markets: Bookstores, jobbers

• WHOLESALERS •

Baker & Taylor Company
W Michael Morris, Asst Buyer
John Cunningham, Children's
  Book Buyer,
Delores Wittemann, Buyer, Small
  and New presses
652 E Main St., PO Box 6920
Bridgewater NJ 08807-0920
908-218-3969
FAX: 908-218-3980
Markets: Bookstores, schools,
  colleges, libraries

Baker & Taylor Company
Donna Lippold, Buyer
Midwest Division
501 S Gladiolus Street
Momence IL 60954-1799
815-472-2444 800-435-1845
FAX: 815-472-4141
Markets: Bookstores, schools,
  colleges, libraries

Baker & Taylor Company
Patricia Bostleman, Buyer
Eastern Division
50 Kirby Avenue
Somerville NJ 08876
908-722-8000
FAX: 908-722-0184
Markets: Bookstores, schools,
  colleges, libraries

Baker & Taylor Company
Jill Bartholomew, Buying Manager
Southeastern Division
Mount Olive Road
Commerce GA 30599-0001
404-335-5000
FAX: 404-335-2027
800-241-6004
Markets: Bookstores, schools, colleges, libraries

Bookazine Company
Fran Stone, Dir of Purchasing
Judy Hayman, Hardcover Buyer
Chris Avena, Paperback Buyer
75 Hook Road
Bayonne NJ 07002
201-339-7777   800-221-8112
FAX: 201-339-7778
Territory: US-IT
Markets: Bookstores, schools, colleges, libraries

Bookpeople
Lisa Mock, Buyer
Sheridan McCarthy, Small Press Titles
Gene Taback, Trade Buyer
7900 Edgewater Drive
Oakland CA 94621-2004
510-632-4700
FAX: 510-632-1281
Markets: Bookstores, colleges, libraries

Brodart
Kathy Johnson, Adult Book Buyer
Wendy Beatty, Juvenile Buyer
Sandra L Rose, Main Book Buyer
500 Arch Street
Williamsport PA 17705-0001
717-326-2461   800-233-8467
FAX: 717-326-6769
Territory: US-IT
Markets: Bookstores, retail outlets, schools, colleges, libraries

De Wolfe & Fiske
Lorna Ruby, Children's Books
Barbara Fonthine, Paperbacks
Ann Ghublikian, Trade Buyer
300 Turnpike Street
Canton MA 02021-2311
617-828-8300
Territory: US-IT
Markets: Bookstores, schools, colleges, libraries, Lauriat's department stores

the distributors
Samamtha Arnold, Small Press Books
Sinda Speckman, Buyer, Trade Books
702 S Michigan
South Bend IN 46601
219-232-8500; 800-348-5200
Markets: Bookstores, colleges

Durkin Hayes Publishing Ltd
Cyril Hayes, President
One Colomba Dr
Niagara Falls NY 14305
716-298-5150
FAX: 716-298-5607
Subjects: Children's books,
fiction
Markets: Bookstores, schools,
public libraries

Duval News Co Inc
Mamie Skinner, Fiction Editor
Gil Brechtel, Exec VP
5638 Commonwealth Avenue
PO Box 61297
Jacksonville FL 32236-1297
904-783-2350
Subjects: General fiction
Markets: Bookstores, colleges,
schools, libraries

Golden Lee Book Distributors
Jean Wahlen, Buyer, Children's
Books
Dennis Haritou, Buyer, Trade
Paperbacks
1000 Dean Street
Brooklyn NY 11238
718-857-6333
FAX: 718-857-5997
Markets: Bookstores, schools,
libraries

Ingram Book Company
Wanda Smith, Buyer, Small Press
Titles
1125 Heil Quaker Boulevard
PO Box 17266
Lavergne TN 37086
615-793-3886
FAX: 615-793-3825
Territory: US
Markets: Bookstores, colleges,
libraries

Inland Book Company
David Wilk, President
Karen Haberfeld, Buyer
140 Commerce Street
PO Box 120470
East Haven CT 06512
203-467-4257
FAX: 203-469-7697
800-243-0138
Subjects: General interest, small
press
Markets: Bookstores, libraries

Koen Book Distributors
Bobbie Combs, Children's Buyer
Sally Lindsay, Head Buyer
10 Twosome Drive
PO Box 600
Moorestown NJ 08057
609-235-4444
FAX: 609-235-6914
800-257-8481
Subjects: General interest, small
press
Territory: East US
Markets: Bookstores, public
libraries

Midwest Library Service
Evelyn Smith, Buyer
11443 St Charles Rock Road
Bridgeton MO 63044-2789
314-739-3100
Subjects: General interest,
technical
Territory: Midwest
Markets: Colleges, libraries

Murder One
Mary Cannon Trone, Buyer
Ford Centre
420 N Fifth Street #458
Minneapolis MN 55401
612-339-7644
Subjects: Mysteries
Markets: Bookstores, libraries

Pacific Pipeline Inc
Marilyn Dahl, Buyer, Mass
    market and Trade books
Helen Ibach, Small Press Buyer
8030 South 228th
Kent WA 98032-1171
206-872-5523
FAX: 206-872-0849
Territory: NW US
Markets: Bookstores, schools,
    colleges, libraries

Small Press Distribution Inc
Steve Dickison, Book Buyer
1814 San Pablo Avenue
Berkeley CA 94702-1624
510-549-3336
FAS: 510-549-2201
Subjects: Humanities, general
    fiction, literary novels, poetry
Markets: Bookstores, schools,
    colleges, libraries

• Independent Distributors

The last list of distributors is of the independent distributors. These are the people who deliver the magazines, the mass-market paperback books and some trade books to local grocery stores, drug stores, mini-marts, and more retail outlets than you can imagine. Sometimes, they are willing to distribute a local publisher's book – depending of course on the type of book you have. *Be sure to contact* each one of these in your area.

I have limited this particular list to Washington and Oregon, but that does not mean that you have to be limited, too. If you live outside this area, check your local phone book for those closest to you and check in the library for those phone books in your state. Or, if you feel that your book has a market in the other states as well, *The Book Publishing Resource Guide by Marie Kiefer, Ad-Lib Publications, 51 1/2 West Adams, PO Box 1102, Fairfield, IA, 52556-1102, (800) 669-0773,* has a complete list of all independent distributors in the U.S. This is a valuable resource and, once again, I strongly urge you to use them.

• WASHINGTON •

Adams News Company Inc
Bob Lofgren, Buyer
1555 W Galer Street
Seattle WA   98119-3128
206-284-7617
FAX: 206-284-7599

ARA Services Magazine & Book
  Division
Paul Onkels, Manager
1419 Hathaway
PO Box 2399
Yakima WA 98907
509-248-7810

ARA Services Magazine & Book
  Division
Bob Reis, Manager
15 Perry St., PO Box 4067
Spokane WA 99202
509-535-3059

Cascade News
Michael J O'Connell, Book Buyer
1055 Commerce Avenue
Longview WA 98632
206-425-2450

Lesnick News Co Inc
Anthony Lesnick, Owner
2442 Mottman Road SW
Tumwater WA 98502
206-357-5341

Pacific Periodical Services
Donna Robertson, Buyer
9914 32nd Ave South (98409)
PO Box 98907
Tacoma WA 98498
206-581-1940

Rainier News Inc
John Thompson, Buyer
1122 80th Street SW
Everett WA 98203-6297
206-355-5350
FAX: 206-355-9833

Servatius News Agency
Fred Servatius, Owner
601 Second Street
Clarkston WA 99403-1995
509-758-7592

Wenatchee News Agency
Jack L Davis, Owner
1501 N. Miller
Wenatchee WA 98801-1513
509-662-3511

• OREGON •

ARA Services Magazine and
  Book Div
Stan Ritari, Manager
3850 W First Avenue
PO Box 15003
Eugene OR 97401
503-484-1300

Bay News Company
John Franznick, Manager
3155 NW Yeon Avenue
Portland OR 97210
503-228-0251

Coos Bay Distributors
Mike Miller, Manager
131 N Schoneman Street
Coos Bay OR 97420
503-888-9203

Corvallis Periodicals
Joseph Meier, Owner
350 Wake Robin Avenue
PO Box 830
Corvallis OR 97339-0830
503-758-0315

Cummings Distributing
Wendy, Manager
1745 23rd Street SE
Salem OR 97302
503-399-7731

FC Himber Sons Books Inc
Dorlon Himber, Owner
1380 W 2nd Avenue
Eugene OR 97402-4190
503-523-7711

Northwest News
Stanley Lakefish, Owner
3100 Murriman Road
Medford OR 97501
503-779-5225

• CHAPTER SEVEN •

BOOKSTORES

Fame is proof that people are gullible.
Ralph Waldo Emerson, (1803 - 1882)

• Bookstore Signings and Readings

Most bookstores are quite supportive of their local authors. Of course, without some prior publicity that you will be signing books at any bookstore, you just might end up sitting at your table, bored and mostly ignored by the few walk-in customers. Or, if you've planned to do a reading, there's nothing more disappointing than coming to a store and having nobody show up. Not only will you be sorely disappointed, but so will the bookstore personnel. A reading means a lot of time and hard work for them, too. For this reason, they may be hesitant about offering to set up a reading or a signing for any new and unknown author.

• Self-Promotion

– NEWSPAPERS AND RADIOS –

The solution and the best way to have a good turn-out at your bookstore readings is to learn to promote yourself. Arrange with the newspapers in your area to have a book review and/or an interview come out the week before your session at the bookstore. Actually, the editors are much more liable to put your review in their paper, or at least a little write-up about you, if they can give their readers a definite time and place to see you. Keep trying until one or more newspapers agree to do this. This can be done with an interesting press release announcing your appearance in regards to your new book. Don't forget to send a press release to all other newspapers in the general area and to the radio stations. Also, ask the bookstore to run an ad – even if you have to offer to split the cost.

If you can tie in a radio interview with a bookstore signing or reading, all the better. A bookstore will usually jump at the prospect of having you in for an autographing session, especially if you promise to mention, on air, the day and time that you will be there. It's free advertising for them, too.

When my first book, *Hayseeds In My Hair*, came out, every trip to downtown Seattle became a book-selling expedition. Also, Bellingham, and Bellevue, and Bremerton. I visited every bookstore, newspaper office, and radio station in every town within a days' drive of my house, thumbing through the yellow pages when I got there to make sure I didn't miss any. Our vacations were also planned around the proximity of bookstores - giving me a chance to pop in and show them the book on the way through town.

Ultimately, I appeared on seven radio talk-shows and had a big fist-full of articles written in local newspapers. And for about a year, the sales on that book were incredible. Three years later, I still meet readers who heard me on one of those shows or read about me in the paper. Most of them eventually bought a copy.

– LIBRARIES –

Libraries can be a gold-mine to any newly-published author. Call the libraries in your area and offer to do a reading. Or teach a class on creative writing or self-publishing. Any reason to send out yet another press release will get your name in front of those media personnel who can make a tremendous difference in your success.

• Mail Directly to the Bookstores

For those bookstores outside your area, whether they are part of a bookstore chain or are an independent, the best way to get the news out that you have published a new book is to notify them through the mail.

Note: See the sub-title below, *Direct Mail Advertising*, under *Independent Distributors*, for even more information on bulk-mailings.

• Bookstore Chains

Below is a list of most of the larger bookstore chains in the nation. You'll want to send each one of them a package containing a book, a cover letter, and a press kit. If you can't afford to give away any more books, at least send the press kit with a book cover.

There are regional buyers for many of the larger companies, such as *B. Dalton* and *Waldenbooks*, and your book will probably wind up on one of their desks. Don't worry about it. Direct your sample copy to the representative who most closely seems in charge of your type of book and hope for the best. From then on, your book will follow certain guidelines known only to those who work there. Though these company policies may seem strange and obscure and your book seems in danger of being

lost forever to red tape, rules and protocol, there are those who understand the processes and will give your book a careful consideration. So, take heart. Even though it may take up to several months, you will almost always, in time, receive a reply. *Be sure to follow-up that mailing with a phone call.*
Note: People are hired and fired and change jobs all the time. When you call, if you can't reach the buyer in the listing, ask to speak to anyone who is a buyer for your type of book. Know what you're going to say — write it down so you won't forget. Be pleasant, professional, but most of all, *be persistent.*

Abranovic Associates
Mary Hritz, Book Buyer
161 South McKean St
Kittanning PA 16201
6 stores

Alaska Natural History
Book Buyer
605 West 4th Avenue #120
Anchorage AK 99501
32 stores

Annie's Book Stop
Annie Adams, Book Buyer
Westwood Plaza
681 High ST #109
Westwood MA 02090
56 stores

Atlantic Bookshops
Michael Carroll, Book Buyer
1036 Bethlehem Pike, Route 309
Montgomeryville PA 18936-9621
5 stores

Barbara Weindling Bookseller
Barbara Weindling, Owner
69 Ball Pond Road
Danbury CT 06811

Barbara's Bookstore
Pat Peterson, Book Buyer
1100 Lake St.
Oak Park IL 60301
4 stores

B Dalton / Barnes & Noble
Sharon Smith, Assistant Buyer
George Greller, Buyer, Astrology,
     Family
Karen Paterson, Buyer, Biography, Mysteries, Westerns
Tom Willshire, Buyer, Business
Gail Doobinin, Buyer,
     Children's Books
Leslie Gareych, Buyer,
     Children's Books
Sarah Erickson, Buyer,
     Children's Books
Lee Stern, Buyer,
     Cookbooks, Health
Linda Braun, Buyer, Fiction,
     Trade & HC
Mike Cavanaugh, Buyer, Juvenile
     Non-book
Cathy Mahar, Buyer, Literature,
     Poetry, History, True Crime
Rick Kenyon, Buyer, Magazines
Glenn Timony, Buyer,
     Psychology, Self-help,
     Recovery, Native-American

Jason Napora, Buyer, Self-
published, Spanish books
122 Fifth Avenue
New York, NY 10011-5605

Bedford Books
Donald Alper, VP
18 Priscilla Lane
Auburn NH 03032
12 stores

Benjamin Books
Deane Kierpa, Book Buyer
330 Dalziel Road
Linden NJ 07036

Black Bond Books
Michael Neill, Book Buyer
14-15531 - 24th Avenue
Surrey V4A 2J4 BC Canada
6 stores

Book Alcove
Carl Sickles, Owner
15976 Shady Grove Road
Gaithersburg MD 20877
2 stores

The Book Cache
Lynn Dixon, Executive Director
325 W Potter Drive
Anchorage AK 99518
14 stores

Book Gallery
Anne McKenzie, Book Buyer
1352 Gaskins Road
Richmond VA 23233

Book Gallery & Restaurant
Jackie McKenzie, Book Buyer
1207 Emmet St
Charlottesville VA 22901
3 stores

Book & Game Company
Shelley Dyer, Book Buyer
Ms Chris O'Hara, Owner
313 W Riverside Avenue
Spokane WA 99201

Book Inventory Systems
Rebecca Riccio, Acquisitions
Amy Cooper, Assistant Manager
5451 S State St
Ann Arbor MI 48108
buys for 26 independent stores

The Book Rack Ltd
Robert W Hugo, Owner
52 State St
Newburyport MA 01950

Book Rack Management
Fred Darnell, Owner
2703 E Commercial Boulevard
Fort Lauderdale FL 33308-4112
200+ stores

Bookland Downtown
David Turitz, Owner
One Monument Way
South Portland ME 04106
2 stores

The Book & Record, Main Office
Georgia Kustas, Owner
Commerce St.
Poughkeepsie NY 12603
3 stores

Book 'N Card Inc
Tom Bonday, Book Buyer
Warwick Village South Center
PO Box 1636
Newport News VA 23601
5 stores

Book Bag Stores
James Joolsby, Manager
2556 Oscar Johnson Dr
PO Drawer 40
Charleston SC 29402-0040
10 stores

Book Corner
Michael Joachim, Book Buyer
512 W Main St
Shrewsbury MA 01545
12 stores

The Book Emporium
Deb Rogers, Book Buyer
1301 SW Washington ST
Peoria IL 61602-1795

Booksellers
Arthur Heuer, Buyer
Wit & Wisdom Inc
24031 Chagrin Boulevard
Beachwood OH 44122

Book World
Andrea Glynn, Manager
3600 N Main St
Rockford IL 61103

Book World Inc
Bill Streur, Book Buyer
2420 West 4th St
Appleton WI 54914-4621

Bookland Stores
Bill Sorensen, Buyer
Geoff Colquitt, Buyer
PO Box 19768
Birmingham AL 35219
99+ stores

Books Connection
Patricia Franks, Book Buyer
55555 Jewell
Shelby Township MI 48315
3 stores

Books Inc
Mike Grant, VP
Corporate Office
120 Park Lane
Brisbane CA 94005
13 stores

The Bookstore Inc
Peter Rossi, Book Buyer
808 Green Avenue
PO Box 1713
Altoona PA 16601-4724
2 stores

BookWorld
Suzanne Shaw, Book Buyer
499 Merritt Avenue
Nashville TN 37203
5 stores

Deseret Book Company
Susan Ingebretsen, Children's
    books
Paul Hastings, Religious Books
James Asay, Trade Book Buyer
40 E South Temple
PO Box 30178
Salt Lake City UT 84130-0178
25 stores

Century Bookstores & Video
    Hdqtr
Kathy Blackmas, Buyer
3915 Camp Bowie
Fort Worth TX 76107

Chicago Tribune Gift Stores
Ken Widelka, Manager
Tribune Tower
435 N Michigan Avenue
Chicago IL 60611-4022
6 stores

A Clean Well-Lighted Place
Ann Seaton, Manager
493 Seaport Court # 105
Redwood City CA 94083
3 stores

Coles Bookstores
Helen Babiak, Book Reviewer
90 Ronson Dr
Etobicoke M9W 1C1 ON Canada
230 stores

Community News Center
John O Stoll, President
2109 Hamilton Road
Okemos MI 48864-1700
9 stores

Community News Center
Robert Morris, Manager
Indiana Periodicals
2120 S Meridian
Indianapolis IN 46225
5 stores

Construction Bookstore
Marilyn Holden, Mgr
29113 Northwestern HWY
Southfield MI 48034

Copperfield's Books
Paul Jaffe, New Book Buyer
138 N Main St
Sebastopol CA 95472

Crown Books
Jeanne Herrick, Softcover Buyer
Corporate Offices
3300 75th Avenue
Landover MD 20785
257 stores

Davis-Kidd Booksellers
Mike Jaynes, Manager
113 N Peters Road
Knoxville TN 37923

Dickens Books Limited
Daniel Goldin, Buyer
409 E Silver Spring Drive
Milwaukee WI 53217

Dickens Books Limited
John E Klund, Book Buyer
415 E Silver Spring Drive
Milwaukee WI 53217
6 stores

Du Bey's News Centers
William DuBey, Buyer
115 S Monroe St
PO Box 11119
Tallahassee FL 32302

Encore Books
Dan Mee, Mass Market Book
    Buyer
Brian Weese, Trade Book Buyer
424 Railroad Avenue
Shiremanstown PA 17011
46 stores

Farley's Books
James H Farley
44 S Main St
New Oxford PA 18938

Godard Stationery Stores
Guillaune Godard, Owner
PO Box 124
Cornwall K6H 5S7 ON Canada
6 stores

Gordon's Booksellers
Debora Kick, Book Buyer
2113 N Charles St
Baltimore MD 21218
8 stores

Graham's Book and Stationery
Teri Graham, Co-Owner
460 Second ST
Lake Oswego OR 97034-3127

Guzzardo's
George Guzzardo, Owner
111 N Main St
Kewanee IL 61443-2221
5 gift stores

Hatch's Bookstores
Robert Hatch, Book Buyer
15677 East 17th Avenue
Aurora CO 80011
10 stores

Hastings Books, Music & Video
Scott Harmon, Book Buyer
Mike Garner, Senior Book Buyer
2101 S Western # 15
Amarillo TX 79109-3267

Hinkle's Inc
Ellen Schultz, Book Buyer
PO Box 2109
Winston-Salem NC 27102-2109
7 stores

Honolulu Book Shops
Colin T Miyabara, Mgr
287 Kalihi St
Honolulu HI 96819
5 stores

Hoover Brothers Inc
Pam Martin, Natl Retail Manager
2050 Postal Way
PO Box 660420
Dallas TX 75266-0420

Hudson News
Mario DiDomizio
1305 Peterson Plank Road
North Bergen NJ 07047
30 dealers

J K Gill
Phil Garrett, Book Buyer
Scholls View Plaza #304
4850 SW Scholls Ferry Road
Portland OR 97225
67 stores

Kroch's & Brentano's
John Norris, Backlist Buyer
Harlin Smith, Buyer
Ray Carrol, Paperback Buyer
29 S Wabash Avenue
Chicago IL 60603-3145
19 stores

Lauriat's Books
Ann Ghublijikian, Book Buyer
Lorna Ruby, Juvenile Buyer
10 Pequot Way
PO Box 9107
Canton MA 02021-2306
30+ stores

Lemstone Book Branch
Rick Regenfuss, Book Buyer
1123 Wheaton Oaks Court
Wheaton IL 60187
51 stores

Liberty House Book Dept.
Beverly Lewis, Buyer
PO Box 2690
Honolulu HI 96845
7 stores

Libreria Giron
Juan Giron, Book Buyer
3547 West 26th St
Chicago IL 60623-3913
6 stores

Lichtman's News and Books
Gerald Ruby, Owner
24 Ryerson Avenue #400
Toronto M5T 2P3 ON Canada
9 stores

Marjen Books
Marshall Miller, Owner
150 Greenleaf Avenue
Portsmouth NH 03801

Mr Paperback Stores
Gary White, Book Buyer
1135 Hammond St
Bangor ME 04401-5705
13 stores

New 'N Novels
Patrick O'Rourke, Owner
2222 Golden Gate Drive
Greensboro NC 27405

Newsboy Books & Video
Jack Gingold, Book Buyer
Pomona Valley News Agency
10736 Fremont Avenue
Ontario CA 91762-3909
6 locations

Newsland
Tom Hines, Manager
215 Washington ST
PO Box 126
Burlington IA 52601-0126
11 stores

Olsson's Books & Records
Jim Tenney, Senior Buyer
1239 Wisconsin Avenue NW
Washington DC 20007
5 stores

On Cue
Kris Church, Book Buyer
7500 Excelsior Boulevard
Minneapolis MN 55426-4503
3 stores

Oxford Book Stores
Lillian Yeilding, Buyer
Rupert LeCraw, Buyer/Owner
360 Pharr Road NE
Atlanta GA 30305
4 stores

People's News & Book Mart
Annette Adams, Manager
406 Market ST
Parkersburg WV 26101-5339
6 stores

Pentos Retailing Group
Book Buyer
Berwick House
35 Livery Street
Birmingham B3 2PB England

Powell's Books
Miriam Sontz, Manager
1005 W Burnside
Portland OR 97209
6 stores

Powell's Books
Carol Woodcock, Manager
8775 SW Cascade Avenue #M6
Beaverton OR 97005

Powell's Books at PDX
Chequeta Nutt, Manager
7000 NE Airport Way
Portland OR 97218

Rainy Day Books
Judy Rieck, Owner
13511 South Mur-Len
Olathe KS 66062

Readmore Bookstores
Joe Kapps, Vice-President
777 W Goodale Boulevard
PO Box 193
Columbus OH 43216
7 stores

Readmore/Miami Valley News
Dave Schere, Book Buyer
2127 Old Troy Pike
PO Box 315, N Dayton Station
Dayton OH 45404
7 stores

Readmore Books
Doris C Gross, Book Buyer
Austin Periodicals
EAgle Boulevard, PO Box 868
Shelbyville TN 37160
8 stores

Readmore Books
James Brunner, Book Buyer
217 Flanders Avenue
PO Box 598
Lima OH 45802-0598
9 stores

Readmore Books
Vernon Clemans, Book Buyer
Austin Periodicals
1051 Husband Road
Paducah KY 42002
3 stores

Readmore Magazines & Books
Cathy Sarcinella, Buying Manager
2560 S Maryland Parkway
Las Vegas NV 89109
5 stores

Rizzoli International Bookstores
Michael Gray, Book Buyer
300 Park Avenue South
New York NY 10010

S & S Bookstore
Sandra Fellman, Buyer
335-A Main St
Farmingdale NY 11735
7 stores

Saint Paul Book & Staionery
Steve Holm, Purchaser
1233 W County Road E
PO Box 64410
Saint Paul MN 55112-0410
12 stores

Sam Weller's Zion Books
Jean McGean, Buyer
254 S Main ST
Salt Lake City UT 84101
3 stores

Scrantom's Book & Stationery
Evan Z Brauer, Pres.
755 Culver Road
Rochester NY 14609

Shinder's Readmore Bookstores
Bob Parker, Book Buyer
733 Hennepin Avenue
Minneapolis MN 55403
13 stores

The Spirit of '76 Bookstore
Robert Hugo, Owner
Pleasant & School Streets
Marblehead MA 01945-0477

Stacey's Bookstore
Sidney Hannon, Book Buyer
581 Market ST
San Francisco CA 94105
4 stores

Strand Book Stores
Fred Bass, Owner
828 Broadway at 12th St
New York NY 10003-4805
4 stores

Taylor's Bookstores
Susan Cramer, Book Buyer, Non-
Fiction
Carla Parker, Children's Books
Becky Gehres, Fiction Buyer
10495 Olympic Drive S #100
Dallas TX 75220
9 stores

Titles Unlimited
Steven Boynton, Buyer
Princeton Business Park
5 Crescent Avenue
Rocky Hill NJ 08553
6 stores

Town Crier Bookstores
Bonnie Edmonds, Manager
1301 SW Gage #120
Topeka KS 66604
5 stores

Trover Shop Books
Joseph Shuman, Book Buyer
221 Pennsylvania Avenue SE
Washington DC 20003
4 stores

Village Green Bookstores
John Borek, Book Buyer
Monroe Book Corp.
766 Monroe Avenue
Rochester NY 14607
4 stores

The Vons Company
Jack Brennan, Buyer
PO Box 3338
Los Angeles CA 90051

Water St Bookstore
Robert Hugo, Owner
Water ST
Exeter NH 03833

Waldenbooks
Sheryl Stebbins, Director of
Merchandising
US MAIL
Merchandise Buying Dept. #51
PO Box 10208
Stamford CT 06904-2218
UPS
Merchandise Buying Dept. #51
201 High Ridge Road
Stamford CT 06905-3417
1000+ stores

W H Smith Bookstores
N Berrisford, Buying Manager
Janet McKaig, Paper Back Buyer
Anne Gardner, Trade Buyer
113 Merton ST
Toronto M4S 1A8 ON Canada
190 stores

Wills Book Stores
Ethel Allen, Book Buyer
103 Longale Road
PO Box 19239
Greensboro NC 27419-9239
7 stores

Wilkie News
Eric S Oda, Manager
101 S Ludlow St
Dayton OH 45402-1891
3 stores

This is a partial list, at best. There are many other specialty stores which also carry books: Religious Bookstores, College Bookstores, Department Stores, Discount Stores, Gift Shops, Drug Stores, and these have not been listed. For a more thorough listing, consult your local library or the *Book Publishing Resource Guide,* by Marie Kiefer. Also see Independent Distributors, Chapter Six.

• Independent Bookstores

Bookstores cannot carry your title if they don't know about it. Even a potential customer will have to hear about it from somewhere. They will then have to be motivated enough to come in to a bookstore, ask specifically for your book, wait for them to look for it and be told they don't have it. And then, with all the patience of Job, take the time to order it from them, sometimes paying for it sight unseen. Otherwise, the publisher (which is you now, remember?) has to tell the bookstores about this new, incredible book just arrived on the market in as interesting a way as possible.

• Trade Shows

The best way to motivate a bookstore to place an order for your book is to attend trade shows. You will meet hundreds of bookstore owners, managers, and employees there. Plus, publisher's reps and distributor buyers. Sometimes, this is the *only* way to get to meet them and show them your book. Check Chapter Five, page 71 for more information on trade shows and a list of addresses.

• Direct Mail Advertising

The next best way is to send the bookstores something in the mail. There are co-ops which are helpful, but they bundle many, many fliers from any self-publisher who has sent their money in, the same as you. Their fliers or their books may not be of the same quality as yours as some may not be totally dedicated to the same amount of excellence as yourself. But, with co-ops, you'll have no choice as to who you'll be bundled with in this mass package of fliers. There is also a list of co-ops on the previous pages with their addresses.

Your other recourse is to send each store your own brochure or postcard. More expensive? You bet. In printing costs and most definitely in postage. But infinitely more effective.

Since I have more than one book published, I used a brochure. If this your first book, you might want to use a postcard. They mail for 19 cents a piece, regular mail, (the last time I checked with the post-office) and they are effective. On one side, have a full color copy of your cover. On the other side, leave room for their address which is to be run off a computer on sticky tape. To the left, have a few quotes ready from those who have read your book (hopefully, you've garnered some magazine or newspaper reviewers by now.) Or, look up the address of several well-known writers well in advance of this mailing and ask if you can send them a copy to read and if they will give you a few quotable remarks.

You can always use bulk mail, which is much less expensive than first class. Of course, you'll have to buy a permit from the post office. Or use someone else's, such as your local Chamber of Commerce, who only needs to give you their OK and their permit number. Or, the neighborhood weekly newspaper office, if they don't mind, and IF you've been diligent about submitting articles, letters to the editor, placed a few display ads, *and made friends*. It's your call. But, however your budget will stretch, those bookstores will HAVE to be informed that your book is out there, or the chance that your book will find its way onto bookstore shelves grows even smaller.

Listed below are some of the largest independent bookstores in the country. It is by no means a comprehensive list but *if you use it as it was intended*, it will get you started. Your local Booksellers Association Trade Show should also have a pretty complete list of bookstores in your area. Don't forget the ABA (American Booksellers Association). They have a membership directory for sale to members and nonmembers. *Be sure to join them, too, and use their membership directories for mailing your brochures.*

• ALABAMA •

Auburn University Bookstore
Margaret Hendricks, Buyer
1360 Haley Center
Auburn AL 36849

Capital Book and News
Cheryl Upchurch, Owner
214 Montgomery Street
Montgomery AL 36104

Little Professor Book Center
Marilyn Szecholda, Owner
10300 Bailey Cove Road
Huntsville AL 35803

• ALASKA •

Baker & Baker Booksellers
Larry & Lynne Baker, Buyers
Eagle Plaza – 418 Third Street
Fairbanks AK 99501

Hearthside Books
Debbie/Susan, Buyers
Nugget Mall
8745 Glacier Hwy
Juneau AK 99801

Kreig's Books
Ray Kreig, Owner
201 Barrow Street # 1
Anchorage AK 99501-2429

Old Harbor Books
Don Muller, Manager
201 Lincoln Street
Sitka AK 99835

• ARKANSAS •

The Book Mark
Denell Whittingham, Buyer
603 Marion Street
Searcy AR 72143

The Book Nook
Mayrene Nelms, Owner
520 B North Greenwood
Fort Smith AR 72901

Book Rack
Kaye McKaskle, Manager
316 West Main
Blytheville AR 72315

The BookStore
Michael Miller, Owner
117 N Jefferson
El Dorado AR 71730

Campus Bookstore
John Griffiths, Buyer
624 W Dickson Street
Fayetteville AR 72701

Curiosity Book Shop
Margaret Luffman, Owner
113 West Walnut
Rogers AR 72756

• ARIZONA •

The Book Mark
Anne Underhill, Buyer
5001 E Speedway
Tucson AZ 85712

Books Etc
John Wehr, Buyer
901 S Mill Avenue
Tempe AZ 85281

Books West Southwest
David Laird, Owner
2452 N Campbell
Tucson AZ 85719

Changing Hands Bookstore
Gayle Shanks, Owner
414 S Mill Avenue # 109
Tempe AZ 85281

Cover To Cover
Maggie Ketring, Owner
4212 W Cactus Road # 1112
Phoenix AZ 85029

Eastside Records
Ben Wood
217 W University Drive
Tempe AZ 85281

Fountain Hills Bookstore
Michele Stumpf, Owner
11819 N Saguaro Boulevard
Fountain Hills AZ 85268

The Haunted Bookshop
Joyce Whaley, Manager
7211 N Northern Avenue
Tucson AZ 84704

Houle's Books
Mark Hollis, Buyer
36 East Camelback Road
Phoenix AZ 85012

Marco Polo & I
Dick Butler, Owner
4743 E Sunrise Drive
Tucson AZ 85718

The Satisfied Mind
John Rordan, Co-Owner
230 S Montezuma
Prescott AZ 86303

Tortuga Books
Allan Haifley / Jennifer
   Newcomb
PO Box 4073
190 Tubac Road
Tubac AZ 85646

Truepenny Books
William Laws
2509 N Campbell Avenue #117
Tucson AZ 85719

• **CALIFORNIA** •

Aardvark Books
John Hadreas, Buyer
2075 Market
San Francisco CA 94114

Alexander Book Company
Michael Stuppin, Manager
50 Second Street
San Francisco CA 94105

Alhambra Book Store
225 E Main Street
Alhambra CA 91801

ASUCLA Bookstore
Richard MacBriar, Trade Buyer
308 Westwood Plaza
Los Angeles CA 90024

Author Author Bookstore
Book Buyer
1218-A Beryl Street
Redondo Beach CA 90277

Avenue Books
Mary & Bob Bermodes, Owners
Lincoln Center South
840 W Benjamin Holt Drive
Stockton CA 95207

Avenue Books
Elise White, Buyer
2904 College Avenue
Berkeley CA 94705

Bay Books
Donna Davison, Buyer
1669 Willowpass Road
Concord CA 94520

Beers Book Center
William Senecal, Manager
1116 15th Street
Sacramento CA 95814-3910

Big & Tall Books
David Erikson, Co-owner
7311 Beverly Boulevard
Los Angeles CA 90036

Black Oak Books
Donald Pretari, Buyer
Robert Brown, President
1491 Shattuck Avenue
Berkeley CA 94709

Blind Moth Books & Drinks
Book Buyer
4029 Ball Road
Cypress CA 90630

Blue Door Bookstore
Tom Stoup, Owner
3823 Fifth Avenue
San Diego CA 92103

Bo Tree Books
Diane Estus, Manager
4005 Govener Drive
San Diego CA 92122

Book Castle
Book Buyer
3604 W Magnolia Boulevard
Burbank CA 91505

Book Emporium
Book Buyer
5539 Stearns Street
Long Beach CA 90815

Book Passage
Julie Duff, Buyer
51 Tamal Vista Boulevard
Corte Madera CA 94925

Book Soup
Glen Goldman, Owner
8818 Sunset Boulevard
West Hollywood CA 90069

The Book Store
Book Buyer
216 Balsam
Ridgecrest CA 93555

Book Warehouse
Mr Fawzi Morrar, Manager
2485 Notre Dame Blvd. #230
Chico CA 95928

Bookends Bookstore
Tom Pieper, Owner
1014 Coombs Street
Napa CA 94559-2587

Bookfriends
Stephanie Mischak, Owner
3610 Sacramento Street
San Francisco CA 94118

The Bookplace
Book Buyer
5769 D East Santa Ana Cyn Road
Anaheim Hills CA 92807

Bookshop Santa Cruz
Judith Milton, Buyer
1547 Pacific Avenue
Santa Cruz CA 95060

Booksmith
Gary Frank, Owner
1644 Haight Street
San Francisco CA 94117

Bookworks
Tom Unsicker, Owner
36 Rancho del Mar Center
Aptos CA 95003

Bookworm of Upland
Joanna Hamilton, Owner
229 N 2nd Avenue
UPland CA 91786

The Bookworm
Mary Littell, Owner
2155 Ventura Boulevard
Camarillo CA 93010

Browser Books
Steven Damon, Owner
2195 Filmore Street
San Francisco CA 94115

Butler & Mayes Booksellers
Jon Mayes, Co-owner
8657 Villa La Jolla #125
La Jolla CA 92037-2391

Caffeine Mary's
Mary Mumford, Owner
52 S Washington ST
Sonora CA 95370

Capitola Book Cafe
Book Buyer
1475 41st Avenue
Capitola CA 95060

Chatterton's Book Shop
William Iwamoto, Owner
1818 N Vermont
Los Angeles CA 90027

Chelsea Bookstore
Scott Walewski, Owner
2501 E Broadway
Long Beach CA 90803

Chevalier's Books
Book Buyer
126 N Larchmont Boulevard
Los Angeles CA 90004

Christopher's Books
Ms Tee Minot, Owner
1400 18th Street
San Francisco CA 94107

City Lights Booksellers & Publ
Paul Yamazaki, Buyer
261 Columbus Avenue
San Francisco CA 94133

A Clean Well-Lighted Place
Leona Weiss, Buyer
601 Van Ness Avenue
San Francisco CA 94102

A Clean Well-Lighted Place
Jude Sales, Buyer
David Shavez, Buyer
2417 Larkspur Landing Circle
Larkspur CA 94939

Cody's Books Inc
Patrick Marks, Buyer
2454 Telegraph Avenue
Berkeley CA 94704

The Cottage Bookshop
Sheryl Cotleur, Manager
1225 4th Street
San Rafael CA 94901

Dana Point Book Store
Charlotte Gellis, Owner
24655 La Plaza
Dana Point CA 92629

Depot Bookstore & Cafe
Korje Guttormsen, Buyer
87 Throckmorton Avenue
Mill Valley CA 94941

Diesel; A Bookstore
Alison Read, Buyer
5820 Shellmound #115
Emeryville CA 94608

Dodds Book Shop
Book Buyer
4818 E Second Street
Long Beach CA 90803

Dutton's Books
Steve Daly, Manager
5146 Laurel Canyon Boulevard
North Hollywood CA 91607-
    3199

Earthling Bookshop
Penny Davies, Owner
1137 State Street
Santa Barbara CA 93101

East Bay Books
Sandy Rockowitz, Manager
1555 Washington Avenue
San Leandro CA 94577

Fahrenheit 451 Books
Dottie Ibsen, Manager
540 South Coast Highway #100
Laguna Beach CA 92651

Franciscan Shops
Bill McMullen, Book Buyer
1650 Holloway Avenue
San Francisco CA 94132

Gallery Bookshop
Anthony Mikask, Owner
319 Kasten Street
PO Box 270
Mendocino CA 95460

Green Apple Books
Richard Savoy, Owner
506 Clement STreet
San Francisco CA 94118

Huntley Bookstore
C Gilmore Buyer
175 E Eighth Street
Claremont CA 91711-3980

II Literature
Barry Fields, Owner
456 S La Brea Avenue
Los Angeles CA 90036

John Cole's Bookshop
Barbara Cole, Owner
780 Prospect Street
PO Box 1132
La Jolla CA 92038

Julian Books
Lois Stitner, Owner
16770 Lakeshore Drive Unit K
Lake Elsinore CA 92530

Kalmin The Bookstore
Mina Lakhani, Owner
81 Calle De Industrias
San Clemente CA 92672

Kepler's Books & Magazines
Karen Pennington, Buyer
1010 El Camino Road
Menlo Park CA 94025-4807

Larry's Book Nook
Larry Sydes, Owner
730-A Bancroft Road
Walnut Creek CA 94598

Levinson's Bookstore
Eric Levinson, Owner
1014 Tenth Street
Sacramento CA 94814

Malibu Books & Company
Book Buyer
23410 Civic Center Way
Malibu CA 90265

Margie's Book Nook
Margie Teeter, Owner
35 N Gay Street
Susanville CA 96130

Modern Times Bookstore
Michael Rosenthal, Manager
968 Valencia Street
San Francisco CA 94110

Moe's Books Inc
M Moskowitz, President
2476 Telegraph Avenue
Berkeley CA 94704-2392

Much Ado About Books
Donna Pohlman, Owner
208 E State Street
Redlands CA 92373

Neighborhood Bookstore
Book Buyer
12133 Victory Boulevard
North Hollywood CA 91601

North Town Books
Jack Hitt, Owner
957 H
Arcata CA 95521

Pacific Bookstore
Lori Moe
11755 Wilshire Boulevard #40
Los Angeles CA 90025

Pendragon Books
Eve Sheehan, Book Buyer
5560 College Avenue
North Oakland CA 94618

Phoenix Books and Records
Kate Rosenberger, Book Buyer
3850 24th Street
San Francisco CA 94114

The Phoenix Bookshop
Michael Goth, Manager
1514 5th Street
Santa Monica CA 90401

Plaza Books
Elizabeth Cupp, Buyer
1111 Pacific Avenue
Santa Cruz CA 95060

Portrait of a Bookstore
J Von Zernick, Owner
10061 Riverside Drive
Toluca Lake CA 91602

Printers Inc
Gerry Masteller, Buyer
310 California Avenue
Palo Alto CA 94306

Readmore Bookstore
Michelle Williams, Owner
121 S School Street
Lodi CA 95240

Riverside Book Center
Book Buyer
3561 Riverside Plaza
Riverside CA 92506

Robbins Bookshop
Pamela Sherman, Buyer
Six Petaluma Boulevard North
Petaluma CA 94952

Sierra Bookshop
Jan Shadoff, President
1072 Emerald Bay Rd.
PO Box 16391
South Lake Tahoe CA 95706

Small World Books
Mary Goodfader, Owner
1407 Ocean Front Walk
Venice CA 90291

Solar Light Books
David Hughes, Book Buyer
2068 Union Street
San Francisco CA 94123

Stanford Bookstore
Mark Ouimet, Buyer
515 Lasuen Street
Stanford University
Stanford CA 94305-3079

Stephens & Company
Harry & Dianne Stephens, Owner
PO Box 3221
Idyllwild CA 92549

Thunderbird Bookshop
John & May Waldroup, Co-
owners
3600 The Barnyard
PO Box 22830
Carmel CA 93922

Tower Books
Micki Grundhoeffer, Manager
MTS Inc
2538 Watt Avenue
Sacramento CA 95821-6392

UCLA Bookstores
Book Buyer
University of California
308 Westwood Plaza
Los Angeles CA 90028

Upchurch-Brown Booksellers
Sandra Gideman, Book Buyer
384 Forest Avenue
Laguna Beach CA 92651

Upstart Crow Bookstore
Book Buyer
Seaport Village
835 W Harbor Drive
San Diego CA 92101

Uptown Book Company
Jette & Bernie Howard, Owners
68 N Washington Street
Sonora CA 95370

Ventura Bookstore
Book Buyer
522 E Main Street
Ventura CA 93001

Vroman's Bookstore
Karen Watkins, Book Buyer
695 E Colorado Boulevard
PO Box 90217
Pasadena CA 91101

Wahrenbrock's Book House
Charles Valverde, Manager
726 Broadway
San Diego CA 92101

Walden Pond Books
Marshall Curatolo, Owners
3316 Grand Avenue
Oakland CA 94610

Warwick's Books
Barbara Christman, Mgr & Buyer
7812 Girard Avenue
La Jolla CA 92037

Wessex Books
Tom Haden, Owner
558 Santa Cruz Avenue
Menlo Park CA 94025

Williams' Book Store
Book Buyer
443 West 6th Street
San Pedro CA 90731

World Book & News
Bernie Weisman/Mark Rose,
  Owners
1652 N Cahnenga Boulevard
Hollywood CA 90028

• COLORADO •

Book Cellar of Crested Butte
Terri Coffey, Owner
326 Elk Avenue
Crested Butte CO 81224

Boulder Bookstore
David Bolduc, Owner
1133 Pearl Street
Boulder CO 80302

Capitol Hill Books
Lois Harvey, Owner
300 E Colfax Avenue
Denver CO 80203

Chinook Bookshop
Richard & Judith Noyes, Owner
210 N Tejon Street
Colorado Springs CO 80903

McKinzey-White Booksellers
Joel McKinzey, Owner
8005 N Academy
Colorado Springs CO 80920

Narrow Gauge Newsstand
Colleen Collins, Manager
604 Main Street
Alamosa CO 81101

Poor Richards
Ed Zasadny, Manager
320 N Tejon
Colorado Springs CO 80903

A Reader's Feast
Robert Aikus, Owner
The Annex
142 Beaver Creek Place
Avon CO 81620

Roundhouse Books
Peter Sullivan, Buyer
526 Main Street
Delta CO 81416

Stone Lion Bookstore
Donna Bathory, Buyer
Old Town Square
106 E Mountain Avenue
Fort Collins CO 80524

The Tattered Cover Bookstore
Margaret Maupin, Buyer,
    Frontlist
1536 Wynkoop Street
Denver CO 80202

• CONNECTICUT •

Barrett Bookstore
David Rose, Owner
1123 High Ridge Road
Stamford CT 06905

Huntington's Bookstores Inc
David Epstein, Owner
65 Asylum Street
Harford CT 06103

Just Books
Warren Cassell, Owner
19 E Putnam Avenue
Greenwich CT 06830

Little Professor Book Centers
Linda Z Deignan, Owner
Fox Run Mall
45 Welles Street
Glastonbury CT 06033

New Canaan Bookshop
Mark Nichols, Buyer
59 Elm Street
New Canaan CT 06840-5499

The Village Bookshop
Denise Austin, Manager
781 Cromwell Avenue
Rocky Hill CT 06067

Yale Co-op
Don Straka, Manager
77 Broadway
New Haven CT 06520

• DELAWARE •

McMahon Books
Steve Straw, Buyer
101 Christiana Mall
Newark DE 19702

• DISTRICT OF COLUMBIA •

Kramerbooks
David Tenney, Owner
1517 NW Conneticut Ave
Washington DC 20036

Politics & Prose
Carla Cohen, Co-owner
5015 Connecticut Avenue NW
Washington DC 20008

Sidney Kramer Books
Lansing Sexton, Buyer
1825 I Street NW
Washington DC 20006

• FLORIDA •

Acorn Books
Jennifer Miller, Owner
7230 W Colonial Drive
Orlando FL 32818

The Book Collection
Doug Elkins, Manager
Mall of the Americas #9
7795 West Flagler
Miami FL 33144

Book Gallery
Kaye Henderson, Manager
1206 N Main Street
Gainesville FL 32601

Books & Books Inc
David & Julius Ser, Owners
296 Aragon Avenue
Coral Gables FL 33134

Books Gallery West
Pat Landis, Co-owner
4121 NW 16th Boulevard
Gainesville FL 32605

College Park Books
Kim Bailes, Linda Dalton,
    Owners
711 W Smith Street
Orlando FL 32804

Eagle Books
Peter Nash, Owner
2446 Northwest 13th Place
Gainesville FL 32605-5144

Haslam's Bookstore
Elizabeth Haslam, Buyer
2025 Central Avenue
Saint Petersburg FL 33713

Vero Beach Book Center
Thomas Leonard, Owner
474 21st Street
Vero Beach FL 32960

• GEORGIA •

Aspen Bookshop
Paul Blicksilver, Owner
5896 Memorial Drive
Stonewood Village Shopping Ctr
Stone Mountain GA 30083

The Book House
Sylvia Thurston, Owner
692 Puckett Drive
Mableton GA 30059

Scitrek Bookstore
Karen Littrel, Owner
395 Peidmont Avenue NE
Atlanta GA 30308

• ILLINOIS •

57th Street Books
Rodney Powell, Book Buyer
1301 East 57th Street
Chicago IL 60637

Book Market
William Linzmeier, Buyer
11138 W Grand Avenue
Melrose Park IL 60164

The Book Market
David Clark, Manager
4018 N Cicero Avenue
Chicago IL 60641

The Book Merchant
Jerry Shirk, Owner
3012 14th Avenue
Rock Island IL 61201

The Bookmark
Diane Butler, Manager
61 Market View Drive
Champaign IL 61820

Books Off Berwyn
Phillip La Palio Jr, Owner
5220 N Clark Street
Chicago IL 60640

Chapter One Bookstore
Patricia & Stuart Gresham,
   Owners
Fairhills Mall
1931 W Monroe
Springfield IL 62704

Guild Books
Richard Bray, Manager
2456 N Lincoln Avenue
Chicago IL 60614

A House of Books
Judy Zindars, Pres.
4812 N Prospect Road
Peoria Heights IL 61614

Northern Light Bookshop
John Mulopulos, Owner
221 W Lincoln
Dekalb IL 60115

Pages for All Ages Bookstore Inc
Brandon Griffing, Manager
1749 W Kirby Avenue
Champaign IL 61821

Powell's Book Store
Book Buyer
1501 East 57th Street
Chicago IL 60637

Powell's Book Store
Book Buyer
2850 North Lincoln
Chicago IL 60657

Powell's Book Store
Book Buyer
828 S Wabash
Chicago IL 60605

Robin's Bookshop Ltd
Mary Lou Burgess, Buyer
220 S Third Street
Geneva IL 60134-2792

Sandmeyers Bookstore
Book Buyer
714 S Dearborn Street
Chicago IL 60605

The Seminary Co-op Bookstore
Jack Cella, Book Buyer
5757 S University Avenue
Chicago IL 60637

Shadid's Book Mart
Woodrow Shadid, Manager
229 S Sixth Street
Springfield IL 62701

Stuart Brent Books
Adam Brent, Buyer
670 N Michigan
Chicago IL 60611

Town House Books
Marilou Kelly, Buyer
105 N Second Avenue
Saint Charles IL 60174

Unabridged Books Inc
Kyle Martin, Manager
3251 N Broadway
Chicago IL 60657

• INDIANA •

The Bookery
Carolyn M Rosetta, Owner
109 W Second Street
Seymour IN 47274

City News & Bookstore
Walter M George Foreman,
Owner
519 S Main Street
Elkhart IN 46516

Corner Book Store
Suzanne Flinn, Manager
2625 W 16th Street
Bedford IN 47421

Howard's Bookstore
Howard & Mary Canada, Owners
101 N College
Bloomington IN 47404

Indiana University Bookstore
Anna Ensley, Trade Buyer
Indiana Memorial Union
Bloomington IN 47405-3201

• IOWA •

Ex Libris Book Store
Eric Adam, Manager
371 Bluff Street
Dubuque IA 52001

Iowa Book & Supply
Matt Lage, Trade Book Buyer
85 Clinton
Iowa City IA 52240

Jim's Books
Jim Holtkamp
2622 Beaver Avenue
Des Moines IA 50310

Prairie Lights Books
Paul Ingram, Book Buyer
15 S Dubuque Street
Iowa City IA 52240

• KANSAS •

Adventure Bookstore
Mary H Michener, Owner
836 Massachusetts Street
Lawrence KS 66044-2658

Bookslinger
Natalie Hougland, Buyer
3814 West 95th Street
Leawood KS 66206

D Martin's Bookshop
Donald Martin
14912 West 87th
Lenexa KS 66215

Great Titles Ltd
Larry & Cindy Mogolov, Owners
11934 Roe Avenue
Overland Park KS 66209

Yellow Brick Road
June Butler, Buyer
206 South Main Street
Ottawa KS 66067

• LOUISANA •

Book Depot Inc
Mickey Deslatte, Co-owner
523 E Ascension Street
Gonzales LA 70737

Book Warehouse
Gerald Phares, Owner
9596 Florida Boulevard
Baton Rouge LA 70815

De Ville Books and Prints
Dave Bruewington, Manager
One Shell Square
109 Concourse
New Orleans LA 70139

McKellar's Books & Gifts
Billy McKellar
3220 Johnston Street
PO Box 3174
Lafayette LA 70503

• MAINE •

Blue Hill Books
Nicholas Sichterman, Owner
2 Pleasant Street
Blue Hill ME 04614

Patricia Buck's Emporium
Patricia Buck, Owner
Main Street
Kingfield ME 04947

Thomaston Book & Prints
Darrilyn Peters, Owner
105 Main Street
Thomaston ME 04861

• MARYLAND •

The Bookstall
Hugo Rizzoli, Owner
10144 River Road
Potomac MD 20854-4903

Chuck & Dave's Books
Charles Dukes, Owner
7001 Carroll Avenue
Takoma Park MD 20912

Cover To Cover Bookstore
Marsha Berman, Manager
7284 Cradlerock Way
Columbia MD 21045

Little Professor Book Center
Billie Germano, Owner
971 C-D Beards Hill Plaza
Aberdeen MD 21001

Louie's Bookstore Cafe
Ann MacKebee, Buyer
518 N Charles
Baltimore MD 21201

Main Street Books
Fred Powell, Manager
Ten E Main Street
Frostburg MD 21532

News Shop
Charles Weaver, Owner
13 S Main Street
North East MD 21901

• MASSACHUSETTS •

Baker Books
Michelle McKay, Buyer
80 William Street
New Bedford MA 02740

Barillari Books
Andy Tand, Book Buyer
One Mifflin Place
Harvard Square
Cambridge MA 02138

Boston University Bookstore
Frank Allen, Buyer
Kenmore Square
660 Beacon Street
Boston MA 02116

Bunch of Grapes
Anne Nelson, Owner
68 Main Street
PO Box 1608
Vineyard Haven MA 02568

Buttonwood Books & Toys
Betsey Detwiler, Buyer
Cusion Plaza
Route 3A
Cohasset MA 02025

Cabbages & Kings
Bess Moyer, Buyer
628 Main Street
Chatham MA 02633

Ernie's Bookland
Ernie Boudreau, Manager
143 Central Street
Lowell MA 01852

Evergreen Books
Lee L Miller, Owner
Two Sudbury Crossing Route 20
Sudbury MA 01776

The Globe Bookshop
Mark Brumberg, Owner
38 Pleasant Street
Northampton MA 01060

Harvard Book Stores
Carole Horn, Buyer
General Offices
1256 Massachusetts Avenue
Cambridge MA 02138

Little Professor Book Center
John Sherman, Owner
1070 Iyanough Road Route 132
Hyannis MA 01601

Mandrake Bookstore
Irwin Rosen, Owner
Eight Story Street
Cambridge MA 02138

Reading International
Chuck Pacheco, Book Buyer
43 Leonard Street
Belmont MA 02178

Reading International
John Netzer, Manager
Wayne A Drugan, Buyer
47 Brattle Street
1280 Massachusetts
Cambridge MA 02138

Sign of the Owl
Sheri Mattison/Joan Melchiono
13 Wianno Avenue
Osterville MA 02655

The Tatnuck Bookseller
Ron Secor, Buyer
647 Chandler Street
Worcester MA 01602

Trident Booksellers
Bernard Flynn, Owner
338 Newbury Street
Boston MA 02115

Wordsworth Bookstore
Donna Friedman, Book Buyer
30 Brattle Street
Cambridge MA 02201-0229

World Eye Bookshop
Antha Smith, Buyer
60 Federal Street
Greenfield MA 01301

• MICHIGAN •

Birmingham Bookstore
Bonnie Weinstein, Owner
263 Pierce Street
Birmingham MI 48009

Bookpeople
Sandra Nathanson, Co-owner
6399 Orchard Lake Road
West Bloomfield MI 48322

Brennen's Book Store
Dennis & Connie Brennen,
  Buyers
530 S Whittaker Street
New Buffalo MI 49117

Cuda's Book Store
Steve Wydendorf, Manager
14310 Michigan Avenue
Dearborn MI 48126

Dobbs-Books Etc
Paul Dobbs, Owner
865 Wing Street
Plymouth MI 48170

Horizon Books
Victor Herman, Owner
224 E Front Street
Traverse City MI 49684

Jocundry's Books
Larry Shields, Book Buyer
515 East Grand River Ave
East Lansing MI 48024

Little Professor Book Center
Richard & Paul Herstein, Owners
37115 Grand River
Farmington MI 48024

Little Professor Book Center
Linda Marl, Manager
Westgate Shopping Center
2531 Jackson Road
Ann Arbor MI 48103

New Horizons Book Shop
Book Buyer
20757 13 Mile Road
Roseville MI 48066

Oak Park Book Center
Book Buyer
23021 Coolidge Hwy
Oak Park MI 48237

Reading Express Book Station
Venita Ciesla, Owner
25812 Middlebelt
Farmington Hills MI 48336

Schuler Books Inc
Brian Younker, Buyer
2975 28th Street SE
Grand Rapids MI 49512

Singapore Bank Bookstore
Judy Hallisy, Owner
317 Butler Street
Saugatuck MI 49453

Wise Owl Book Shoppe
Book Buyer
25873 Ford Road
Dearborn Heights MI 48127

Young & Welshans
Joan Chapman, Manager
Sommerset Town Centre
4270 Miller Road
Flint MI 48507

• MINNESOTA •

Baxter's Books
Brian & Carol Baxter
North Star East #129
608 Second Avenue S
Minneapolis MN 55402

The Bookcase
Peggy Burnet, Owner
607 E Lake Street
Wayzata MN 55391

Borders Bookshop
Calhoun Square
3001 Hennepin Avenue S
Minneapolis MN 55408

Carleton College Bookstore
Harriet Pierce, Manager
One N College Street
Northfield MN 55057

Gringolet Books
Mike Leimer, Co-Owner
125 Main Street SE
Minneapolis MN 55414

Hungry Mind Bookstore
David Unowsky, Owner
1648 Grand Avenue
Saint Paul MN 55105

Koehler Book & Stationery
Forrest Watson, Owner
206 Bush Street
Red Wing MN 55066

Lake Country Booksellers
Persis Fitzpatrick, Manager
4766 Washington Square
White Bear Lake MN 55110

Micawber's Bookstore
Margaret Nelson, Buyer
2238 Carter Avenue
Saint Paul MN 55108

Odegard Books
Book Buyer
Centennial Lakes Plaza
7505 France Avenue South
Edina MN 55435

Odegard Books of Saint Paul
Lisa Hamnes & Frank Randall
857 Grand Avenue
Saint Paul MN 55105-3377

Orr Books
Charlie Orr, Owner
3043 Hennepin Avenue S
Minneapolis MN 55408

SCS University Stores
R V Ward, Buyer
Saint Cloud University
801 2nd Avenue South
Saint Cloud MN 56301

• **MISSISSIPPI** •

Lemuria Bookstore
John Evans, Owner
202 Banner Hall
4465 I-55 North
Jackson MS 39206

Square Books
Richard Howerth, Owner
On The Square
1126 Van Buren Avenue
Oxford MS 38655

• **MISSOURI** •

A to Z Books
Debbie Welch, Book Buyer
1400 West Highway 40
Blue Springs MO 64015

Anderson's Bookshops Inc
William Anderson, Owner
5429 Antioch Center Mall
Kansas City MO 64119

Bennett Schneider Inc
Hilda Dutton, Buyer
300 Ward Parkway
Kansas City MO 64112

Book Shop at Brookside
Roy & Sandra Beaty, Owners
116 West 63rd Street
Kansas City MO 64113

Left Bank Books Inc
Dale Woolery, Buyer
399 N Euclid
Saint Louis MO 63108

The Library Ltd
Allen & Terry Mittleman, Owners
7700 Forsyth
Clayton MO 63105

Whistler's Books
Michael Chaffee, Manager
427 Westport Road
Kansas City MO 64111

• MONTANA •

Barjon's Books
Barbara E Shenkel, Owner
2718 Third Avenue N
Billings MT 59101-1929

Big Sky Books
Kathryn Holt, Manager
525 Second Avenue
Havre MT 59501

Books & Books
Joe Antonioli, Owner
206 W Park Street
Butte MT 59701

Bookworks
Jack Garlitz, Owner
110 Central Avenue
Whitefish MT 59937

Country Bookshelf
Mary Jane DiSanti, Owner
28 West Main Street
Bozeman MT 59715

Fact & Fiction
Barbara Theroux, Buyer
216 W Main Street
Missoula MT 59802

Freddy's Feed & Read
Ann Bensen, Buyer
1221-3 Helen Avenue
Missoula MT 59801-4491

Gallery Books & Cards
Danita Twedt, Owner
508 W Main Street
Lewistown MT 59457

• NEBRASKA •

Afterthoughts
Curt Olson, Owner
c/o Coffee House
1324 P Street
Lincoln NE 68508

The Book Category
Vicki Wiese, Manager
10323 Pacific Street
Omaha NE 68114

Combs & Combs Bookstore
Barry Combs, Co-owner
11009 Elm Street
Omaha NE 68144

Ketterson's Old Market Book-
store
Andy Ketterson, Co-Owner
1202 Howard Street
Omaha NE 68102
Kieser's Bookstore
George Kieser, Owner
312 S 15th Street
Omaha NE 68102-2207

• NEVADA •

Bold Print Bookstore
Book Buyer
3432 Lakeside Drive
Reno NV 89509

Bookmongers
Leslyn & Chuck Thomas, Owners
940 W Moana Lane # 102
Reno NV 89509

Culture Dog Books
Book Buyer
4350 E Sunset Road # 108
Green Valley NV 89014

Dana McKay Books
Dana McKay, Owner
953 E Sahara
Las Vegas NV 89104

Ensign Bookstore
Mari Lynn Hales, Buyer
640-A N Eastern Avenue
Las Vegas NV 89101

Sandy's Book Shoppe
Sandra E Wickman
1319B Nevada Hwy
Boulder City NV 89005

Solomon Gundy's Book World
Sol & Elaine Levco, Owners
1442 E Charleston Boulevard
Las Vegas NV 89104

Sundance Books
Book Buyer
1155 West 4th Street #106
Reno NV 89503

• NEW HAMPSHIRE •

Apple Tree Book Shop
Eric Griffel, Owner
24 Warren Street
Concord NH 03301

Chapter One Bookstore
Tom Hayes, Co-Owner
650 Elm Street
Manchester NH 03101

Dartmouth Bookstore
Book Buyer
33 S Main
Hanover NH 03755

Little Professor Book Center
Jerome/Barbara Smith, Owners
Worth Plaza
103 Congress Street
Portsmouth NH 03801

Toadstool Bookshop
Holly Williams, Book Buyer
12 Depot Square
Peterborough NH 03458

• NEW JERSEY •

Book World
Stanley Sabin, Owner
895 Bloomfield Avenue
West Caldwell NJ 07006

Cranford Bookstore
Ms Meryl Layton, Owner
32 North Avenue West
Cranford NJ 07016

A Likely Story
Ms Meryl Layton, Owner
Sayerbrook Town Center
2909 Washington Road #25
Parlin NJ 08859

Little Professor Book Center
Mike & Susan Cullis, Owners
Bradlee's Grand Union
S/CTR Rte 35
Middletown NJ 07748

Martine Avenue Bookstore
Ms Meryl Layton, Owner
40 S Martine Avenue
Fanwood NJ 07023

Quimby Street Bookshop
Ms Meryl Layton, Owner
109 Quimby Street
Westfield NJ 07090

Town Bookstore Inc
Marie Laessig, Manager
233 E Broad Street
Westfield NJ 07090

Watchung Booksellers
Cathy Linsk & Lisa Knowlton
33 Watchung Plaza
Montclair NJ 07042

Wit & Wisdom Booksellers
Roger Williams, Owner
160 Lawrence Penn Road
Lawrenceville NJ 08648

• NEW MEXICO •

Bridge Street Book
Peter Dumont & Anne Stevenson
131 Bridge Street
Las Vegas NM 87701

Garcia Street Books
Greg Olson, Owner
376 Garcia Street
Santa Fe NM 87501

Living Batch Ltd
Pat Nelson, Manager
106 Cornell Drive SE
Albuquerque NM 87106

Los Llanos Bookstore
Marjorie Cate, Owner
500 Montezuma
Santa Fe NM 87501

Moby Dickens
Arthur & Susan Bachrack, Buyers
#6 John Dunn House
124A Bent Street
Taos NM 87571

Old Santa Fe Trail Books
Tonja Gould, Owner
613 Old Santa Fe Trail
Santa Fe NM 87501

Page One Bookstore
Angie McCafferty, Book Buyer
11200 Montgomery Blvd NE
Albuquerque NM 87111
Read On!
Forrest Furman, Manager
10200 Corrales Road NW
Albuquerque NM 87048

Salt of the Earth Books
Mimi Wheatwind, Buyer
2128 Central SE
Albuquerque NM 87106

• **NEW YORK** •

The Bashful Bear Bookstore
David Cross, Owner
Water Street
PO Box 614
Elizabethtown NY 12932

Book House of Stuyvesant Plaza
Susan Novotny, Owner
Stuyvesant Plaza
Albany NY 12203-3586

Bookforum
Cliff Fimms, Buyer
2955 Broadway
New York NY 10025-7895

Bookmarks
Sany Van Wormer, Buyer
32 E Market Street
Corning NY 14830-2686

Bookmart
Carmine Lepore, Buyer
253 S William Street
Newburgh NY 12550

Books 'N Things
Charles & Diane Newman,
    Owners
1868 Pleasantville Road
Briarcliff Manor NY 10510

Burlington Bookshop
Jane Trichter, Owner
1082 Madison Avenue
New York NY 10028

Coliseum Books Inc
George Liebson, Book Buyer
1771 Broadway
New York NY 10019

Community Bookstore Park
Susan Scioli, Owner
143 Seventh Avenue
Brooklyn NY 11215

Dolphin Book Shop
Patricia Vunk, Owner
941 Port Washington Boulevard
Port Washington NY 11050

ELIMU
Geneva Hudson, Owner
10 Sickle Avenue
New Rochelle NY 10801

Endicott Booksellers
Stuart Bernstein, Buyers
450 Columbus Avenue
New York NY 10024

Madison Avenue Bookshop
Arthur Loeb, Owner
833 Madison Avenue
New York NY 10021

Printed Matter Bookstore
Book Buyer
77 Wooster Street
New York NY 10012

Putnam Book Center
Hank Jones, Buyer
Putnam Plaza Route 6
Carmel NY 10512

Saint Mark's Bookshop
Robert Contant/David Bowman
12 Saint Mark's Place
New York NY 10003

Shakespeare & Co
Linda Marotta, Book Buyer
Tim Foster, Trade Buyer
2259 Broadway
New York NY 10024

Spring Street Books
Israel Jaronowski, Owner
169 Spring Street
New York NY 10012

Talking Leaves
Jonathan Welch, Manager
3144 Main Street
Buffalo NY 14214-1311

Unity Book Center
Mavis Ueberall, Book Buyer
237 West 23rd Street
New York NY 10011

Village Book Shop
Marianne & David Carlson,
    Owners
77 Purchase Street
Rye NY 10580

• NORTH CAROLINA •

Bull's Head Bookshop
Erica Eisdorfer, Manager
CB 1530 Daniels Building
122 Abernathy Hall 002A
Chapel Hill NC 27514

Bush Stationers Inc
Virginia Bush, Buyer
Cotswald Mall
Charlotte NC 28211

Island Ragpicker
Dorothy Perkins, Buyer
Hwy 12 Box 5
Ocracoke Island NC 27960

The Muses Bookstore
Shirley Sprinkle, Owner
West Union Street
Morganton NC 28655

The Regulator Bookshop
John Valentine, Owner
720 Ninth Street
Durham NC 27705

• NORTH DAKOTA •

Green Mountain Book
Bob Cuskelly, Manager
Po Box 147
Dickinson ND 58601

Wordsworth Books on Broadway
Pat Wold
111 N Broadway
Fargo ND 58102

• OHIO •

Adamy Books
Ellen Ackerman, Co-owner
118 West Streetsboro Road
Hudson OH 44236

The Book Merchant
Mary Lou Ferris, Owner
1127 Euclid Avenue
Cleveland OH 44115

The Bookhound
Barbara Hiney, Buyer
Quaker Square, 120 E Mill Street
Akron OH 44308

Books & Company
Annye Camara, Buyer
350 E Stroop Road
Dayton OH 45429

Browse Awhile Books
William A Jones, Owner
118 E Main Street
Tipp City OH 45371

Chagrin Book Barn
Patricia Haber, Buyer
40 W Orange Street
Chagrin Falls OH 44022

Mother O'Riley's Books
Elin Jones, Owner
232 Market Avenue N
Canton OH 44702-1492

Newton's Book Store
Gary Newton, Owner
Country Square Shopping Center
320 W National Road
Englewood OH 45322

Nickleby's Book Store
Palmer R Cook, Owner
1425 Grandview Avenue
Columbus OH 43212

• OKLAHOMA •

The Book Seller
Sarah Raupe, Owner
124 N Second Street
Guthrie OK 73044

Brace Books & More
Jean Brace, Manager
2205 North 14th Street
Ponca City OK 74601

Cambridge On Brookside
Jane Vogel, Owner
1309 E 35th Street
Tulsa OK 74105

Oklahoma Book Warehouse Inc
Steve C Greenfield, Owner
PO Box 756
Broken Arrow OK 74133

Yorktown Alley Bookstore
Ken Tracy, Manager
3103 South Harvard
Tulsa OK 74135

• OREGON •

Bookshelf
Tracy & Sandra Abernathy,
    Owners
PO Box 4428
Sunriver OR 97707

Catbird Seat Bookstore
Deborah Robbey, Owner
913 SW Broadway
Portland OR 97205-3014

Harvest Book Shoppe
Judith Lovell, Owner
307 Central
Coos Bay OR 97420

Looking Glass Bookstore
Bill Kloster, Buyer
318 SW Taylor Street
Portland OR 97204

Marketplace Books
Karen Swank, Buyer
Fifth Street Public Market
296 East 5th Avenue NBU 8-10
Eugene OR 97210

Twenty Third Avenue Books
Robert Maull, Owner
1015 NW 23rd Avenue
Portland OR 97210

• PENNSYLVANIA •

Ann Ar Bookshoppe
Leslie Bowen, Book Buyer
827 West Linden Street
Allentown PA 18101-1290

Black Mountain Books
Dianne Youells, Manager
Country Club Shopping Center
Route 309
Dallas PA 18612

The Book Keeper Bookstore
Susan Allaire, Owner
1516 Paoli Pike
West Whester PA 10380

Books & Company
Judith Kramer, Owner
781 Huntingdon Pike
Rockledge PA 19111

Bookworks Inc
John Trowle, Manager
1139 Freeport Road
Pittsburgh PA 15238

Das Bookhaus
E Rhoads, Owner
Quakertown Plaza Shopping Ctr.
Route 309
Quakertown PA 18951

Kenny's News Agency & Bookstore
Barbara Kenny Dommel, Owner
17 W State Street
Doylestown PA 18901

News Center West, Offices
Elizabeth Hester, Book Buyer
224 West Shore Plaza
Lemoyne PA 17043

Readers' Forum
Book Buyer
116 N Wayne Avenue
Wayne PA 19087

Robin's Bookstore
Larry Robin, Owner
108 S 13th Street
Pholadelphia PA 19017

• SOUTH CAROLINA •

BestSellers
Robert J McGraw, Owner
7743 N Kings Highway
Myrtle Beach SC 29572

Chapter Two Bookstore
Susan Davis, Owner
199 E Bay Street
Charlestown SC 29401

Conway Book Stop
Ron Morrison, Owner
324 Main Street
Conway SC 29526

The Happy Bookseller
J Rhett Jackson, Owner
4525 Forest Drive
Columbia SC 29206

• TENNESSEE •

Barrett & Co Booksellers
Ms Barrett Brewer, Owner
820 Broad Street
Chattanooga TN 37402

Burke's Bookstore
Corey Mesler, Buyer
1719 Poplar Avenue
Memphis TN 38104

Village Book Shoppe
Gayle Jones, Owner
Athens Plaza
Athens TN 37303

White Rose Books
John Patterson, Owner
65 Monroe Avenue
Memphis TN 38103

• TEXAS •

Barber's Bookstore
Brian Perkins, Owner
215 West 8th Street
Fort Worth TX 76102-6105

Book Gallery
Mark McBrayer, Owner
4310 82nd Street K #230
Lubbock TX 79423

Book People
Paul Sansone, President
4006 South Lamar #250
Austin TX 78704

Books & More
Lawrence Whiddon
3418 Western
Amarillo TX 79109

The Bookstore on Main Street
Tracy Eubanks, Manager
1134 W Main Street
Lewisville TX 75067

Brazos Bookstore
Karl Kilian, Manager
2421 Bissonnet Street
Houston TX 77005

Colloquim Books
Michael Kiely
320 University Drive
San Marcos TX 78676

Congress Avenue Booksellers
Alice R Gaffney, Manager
718 Congress Avenue
Austin TX 78701

Copperfield's
Evelyn Farrell, Owner
1840 Lee Trevino Boulevard
  #106
El Paso TX 79936

Debbie's Book Gallery
Debbie Simmons, Owner
780B NE Alsbury Boulevard
Burleson TX 76028

San Houston Bookshop
Greg Newton, Manager
5015 Westheimer
Houston TX 77056

Spectrum Bookstores Inc
Robert Alexander, Book Buyer
5868 Westheimer
Houston TX 77057

Whole Earth Provision
Don Harris, Manager
2410 San Antonio Street
Austin TX 78705

• UTAH •

The King's English
Elizabeth Burton, Owner
1511 South 15th E
Salt Lake City UT 84105

Valley Book Center
Joan Walters, Owner
52 W Center Street
Provo UT 84601

Waking Owl Books
Nancy Rosen, Buyer
208 South 13th East
Salt Lake City UT 84102

• VERMONT •

Barleby's Books & Music
Peter Herrick, Owner
N Main Street
PO Box 809
Wilmington VT 05363

Book Cellar
Pierre & Betsy Bonin, Owner
120 Main Street
Brattleboro VT 05301

Chassman & Bem Booksellers
Gary Chassman, Owner
One Church Street
Burlington VT 05401

New England Book Service
Dee Morrow
Prindle Road
RR #1 Box 1823
Charlotte VT 05445

Northshire Bookstore
Sandy Lincoln, Buyer
PO Box 2200
Manchester Center VT 05255

Vermont BookShop Inc
Grant Novak, Buyer
38 Main Street
Middlebury VT 05753-1416

• VIRGINIA •

Best Seller
Beth Thompson, Owner
29 W Nelson Street
Lexington VA 24450

Chesapeake Books
Brenda Snively, Owner
701J N Battlefield Boulevard
Chesapeake VA 23320

Chris Huffman Books
Chris Huffman, Buyer
1423 W Main Street
Richmond VA 23220

Horizon Books
Jamie King, Owner
901 W Broad Street
Waynesboro VA 22980

Bailey/Coy Books
Barbara Bailey & Micheal Coy
414 E Broadway
Seattle WA 98102

Bek's Bookstore
Marty Bucher, Buyer
Washington Mutual Tower
1201 3rd Avenue
Seattle WA 98101

Bek's Bookstore
Tom Orton, Manager
Rainier Square Concourse
1301 5th Avenue
Seattle WA 98101

Books on Broadway
Michelle Bielat, Owner
1339 Commerce Avenue
Longview WA 98632

The Bookshop
Dean & Caroline Wood, Owner
1203 14th Avenue
Longview WA 98632

City News
Haricklia Bryant, Owner
10116 NE 8th
Bellevue WA 98004

DeGraff Books
DeGraff Berkey, Buyer
1602 Post Alley
Seattle WA 98101

DeGraff Books
John Siscoe, Manager
999 Third Avenue
Seattle WA 98104

Elliott Bay Book Company
Margaret Nevinski, Buyer
Rick Simonson, Trade Book
  Buyer
101 S Main Street
Seattle WA 98104

Island Books
Ruthanna Bayless, Owner
3014 78th Avenue SE
Mercer Island WA 98040

Kay's Bookmark
Kay Edwards, Owner
2684 NE University Village Mall
Seattle WA 98105

M Coy Books
Michael Coy, Owner
117 Pine
Seattle WA 98101

Madison Park Books
4105 E Madison
Seattle WA 98122

Parkplace Book Co
Kristine Kaufman, Buyer
348 Parkplace Center
Kirkland WA 98033

Puss'N Books
Magda Hitzroth, Owner
15788 Redmond WAy
Redmond WA 98052-3830

Shorey Bookstore
John W Todd Jr, Owner
1411 First Avenue
Seattle WA 98101

University Book Store
Mark Mouser, Buyer
4326 University Way NE
PO Box C50009
Seattle WA 98105-1005

University Book Store
Nicky Markey, Buyer
990 102nd Avenue NE
Bellevue WA 98004

Village Books
Krista Hunter, Buyer
1210 11th Street
Bellingham WA 98225

• WISCONSIN •

Audubon Court Books
Jerry Ellis, Buyer
383 W Brown Deer Road
Milwaukee WI 53217

Book Worm
Rhonda Sherwood, Owner
5433 Park Street
PO Box 343
Boulder Junction WI 54512

The Bookstore
Janice Dooley, Manager
1032 Lincoln Avenue
Sheboygan WI 53081

Brown's Bookshop
Richard Rust, Manager
673 State Street
Madison WI 53703-1089

Conkey's Bookstore
John Zimmerman, Buyer
226 E College Avenue
Appleton WI 54911-5789

Rainbow Bookstore
Marsha Rummel, Manager
426 W Gilman Street
Madison WI 53703

Webster's Books Inc
Tim Wagner/Bill Domer, Co-
    Owners
2559 N Downer Avenue
Milwaukee WI 53211

• WYOMING •

Books-A-Go-Go
James Mason, Owner
408 University Avenue
PO Box 670
Laramie WY 82070

Serendipity Bookstore
Judy Brannan, Buyer
163 South Fifth Street
Lander WY 82520

• DISCOUNT STORES

These stores don't buy from everyone. When they do, they prefer to order directly from the publisher, negotiating a contract based on discount prices. But when they do buy, they buy big! Some of these are:

Advanced Marketing Services
5880 Oberlin Drive #200
San Diego, CA 92122-9653;
(619) 457-2500; (800) 695-3580; Fax: 619-452-0532

Levy Home Entertainment
4201 Raymond Drive
Hillside, IL 60162-1786
(708) 547-4400; (800) 947-1967; Fax: 708-547-4503

Handleman National Book Distributors
500 Kirts Boulevard
Troy, MI 48084
(313) 362-4400; (800) 767-7033; (313) 362-3615

Supermarket Book Distributors
Scott Hurley, Buyer
Center Point Industrial Park
12 S Middlesex Avenue
Cranbury, NJ 08512-9556
(609) 655-8335; Fax: (609) 655-3524

Target Stores
Susan Masko, Book Buyer
33 South 6th Street
Minneapolis MN 55420
(612) 370-6365; Fax: (612) 370-8770

Western Merchandisers
Corey Godfrey, Small Vendors (buyer)
421 East 34th Street
PO Box 32270
Amarillo, TX 79120-2270
(806) 376-6251; (800) 999-0904, Code, 0535
Fax: (806) 379-8731 (Book buyer for Walmart)

Costco Wholesale
Penny Clark, Book Buyer
10809 120th Avenue NE
Kirkland, WA 98033
(206) 828-8100; Fax: (206) 828-8101

• THE MILITARY MARKET

Stars and Stripes Book Department
Pacific Stars & Stripes
APO, AP 96337
(03) 401-8928; Fax: (03) 408-8936

Stars and Stripes Book Department
Europe Stars & Stripes
201 Varick #638
New York, NY 10014-4811
(212) 620-3333; Fax: (212) 620-3268

M.J. Daniel Company
1000 Beltline Road
Carrollton, TX 75006
(214) 245-3600

Army and Air Force Exchange Service
Liz Burkepile, Book Buyer
AAFES Headquarters
Department PD-C Stationery
3911 S. Walton Walker
Dallas TX 75236-1598; (214) 312-2011
Write to Public Affairs Division for free copy, *AAFES Facts for Vendors.*

American Passage
215 W Harrison
Seattle WA 98119
(206) 282-8111; (800) 426-5537; Fax: (206) 282-1280
This company can help you advertise in military base weeklies and college newspapers.

• LIBRARIES

Next to bookstores, libraries are a major market. But you don't want to take them for granted. Their business must be wooed the same as any sale to a bookstore, even though they work in a little different way.

A good review in publications such as: *Publishers Weekly, Library Journal, Booklist, Kirkus Reviews, Choice, Horn Book, School Library Journal,* and *Small Press Book Review* should get the attention of most librarians. If that review fails to appear, you might consider purchasing a small display ad. Yes, it does cost, but many publishers see this expense as a necessary investment. It does tend to validate their title and their company name and give them a degree of credibility that they may not get in any other way. Copies of this ad will also look great in your press kit.

Libraries buy, almost always, from wholesalers. The reason for this is very similar to the reason why bookstores buy from distributors. Convenience (which means one-stop shopping and less paperwork) better and more reliable service, bigger discounts and a wider variety of titles.

But the biggest reason, probably, is the cataloging cards. Libraries must have these cards before they can stock a book on their shelves. When they are offered the card free with an order of the book, it saves the librarian the time it would take to look up the cataloging number and type up the card. Definitely a good selling tool.

These cards can be ordered from the Library of Congress. Write the *Cataloging Distribution Service, Library of Congress, Washington D.C. 20541,* for information on how to get your LCCN (Library of Congress Cataloging Number) and a sample of the cataloging cards. These cards can be printed locally and included in your mail-out to the libraries.

Baker & Taylor is the major wholesaler to libraries. They catalog every new title they stock. In fact, because B & T has made ordering from them such a convenience, some libraries will not order a book which is not available through their system.

In addition to the cards, Baker & Taylor has what they call their Final Approval Program. In this, every title has been reviewed and approved by some very enlightened and savvy staff members for their recommendation to the libraries. Some libraries consider this all the convincing they need and will give that book the nod, almost automatically.

Please, don't let this servicing company scare you away from doing your own direct mail advertising to libraries. Your brochure may be just the thing to motivate them to buy, even though they may actually order the book from a wholesaler. Perhaps an even better way would be to request that B & T give your book serious consideration into their Final Approval Program. For a more complete description of Baker & Taylor, and their addresses, read the information on Baker & Taylor in Chapter Six, Distributors and Wholesalers.

Obtaining the CIP data – the Library of Congress' Cataloging in Publication program – is crucial to selling to libraries and, consequently, being accepted for distribution through Baker & Taylor. By working with their bookkeeping and cataloging system, you're saving the libraries time and extra work. Which means that they are usually much more likely to order your book. See Chapter One for more information on the CIP program.

Any time you're mailing a press release or brochure to libraries, be sure to include the data that is important to them. Author credentials are a big plus. If you're an expert in your field, tell them. Also, does this book have hard or soft-cover or special library bindings? They'll also want to see the ISBN numbers, the LCCN numbers, the publication dates, copyright dates, price, and a short description. Again, see Chapter One for ordering information. Be sure to list the library wholesalers and distributors that carry them.

Consider exhibiting your book at the major library association shows. If this is too expensive, try one of the co-ops. *COSMEP Exhibit Service, PO Box 703, San Francisco, CA 94101-0703,* and *Publishers Marketing Association (PMA) 2401 Pacific Coast Hwy., Ste. 102, Hermosa Beach, CA 90254,* are two of the most well-known. Two other distributors who specialize in marketing to libraries are:

Quality Books
918 Sherwood Drive
Lake Bluff, IL 60044-2204
(708) 295-2010; Fax: (708) 295-1556
(Nonfiction, only)

Unique Books
Richard Capps, Product Manager
4200 Grove Avenue
Gurnee, IL 60031
(708) 623-9171; (708) 623-7238

Penny Lent, of Kaleidoscope Press, (Puyallup, WA), started out as a self-publisher when she found a great need existed for the kindergarten through college-age writers. Though there are many "Young Authors" programs and the national "Reflections" program, there seemed to be nothing available for young people by which they could market their books.

Voila! Penny had found her "niche." She decided not only to research and write the book, but to publish it as well.

Since then, Penny has published nine books in 18 months, which includes a number of projects for other authors. She stresses the importance of the ISBN and the CIP program as a *must* – prior to publication. Naturally, since many of her books are used as research material, school and public libraries are some of her biggest markets.

• Selling Textbooks For Classroom Use

Interested in selling textbooks to schools and colleges? You'll have to convince the teachers that your book is superior to any others they might use, as they are the ones most responsible for the classroom agenda. Therefore, most of them are very open to suggestions on how to improve the quality of their teachings.

Note: John Kremer, in his book, *1001 Ways to Market Your Books,* advises a small publisher to buy a mailing list of schools and teachers. But, he says, don't give away too many complimentary copies. He has had a number of complaints as to these books being sold to used-book wholesalers who resell them to college bookstores and students. For more information, see the above-mentioned book by John Kremer.

Two such mailing list companies are;

Bowker Mailing Lists,
R.R. Bowker Company
245 West 17th Street
New York, NY 10011
(212) 337-7164; Fax: (212) 463-6631

American Library Association
50 E Huron Street
Chicago, IL 60611
(312) 944-6780; (800) 545-2433;
Fax: (312) 440-9374

• FAIRS AND FESTIVALS

When I self-published my first book, *Hayseeds In My Hair,* I was an unknown author. No one had ever heard of me. The few local bookstores that were willing to carry my title did so on a consignment basis only. The sales were sluggish, to say the least. In looking for a more productive and immediate market, I turned to the local county fairs and festivals.

Luckily, I'm married to man who's quite handy with a nail and hammer. He agreed to build me a portable, mini-bookstore that could be easily lifted onto the back of our pick-up and carried from one area to another. This wooden structure, made out of plywood and a lot of paint, sports a roof, walls with shelves on the inside, and a countertop across the front. I took this booth to every fair and festival within a reasonable driving distance, for the first three years my books were out. The arts and craft shows worked very well, especially around Christmas time.

Although it was a lot of work – some days I worked 10 to 12 hours at a stretch – I made a lot of contacts and a little money right off the bat by selling my books at the full retail price directly to my buying public. The customers seemed delighted to meet a "real" author and I got to feel like a "real" author. I autographed books on the spot and answered a lot of questions.

The fairs and festivals also provided me with a measure of instant recognition and gave me a ready market to use time and time again. My own list of customer names for direct mailing. And let us not forget those hundreds of other people who came by my booth but, for one reason or another, did not buy my book at the time of the fair. Some of them gave me their names and some did not, but they are still valuable contacts. They've met me, they've seen my books, and will probably recognize them whenever my books are displayed in a bookstore, mentioned in a review or a newspaper article, or hear me in a radio or T.V. interview.

Note: A good source for the festivals and fairs in Washington State is the *Washington Festival Directory and Resource Guide*, produced by

Northwest Folklife
305 Harrison Stree
Seattle,WA 98109
(206) 684-7300

If you live outside this area, try your local Chamber of Commerce.

• RADIO AND TELEVISION INTERVIEWS
Probably the best way to get an interview is to ask for one. As with the newspapers, you'll probably want to start with the local stations. Call them and ask for the name of the disc jockey who does their interviews. Then ask to speak with her or him. If she's on the air at that time, or not in, ask for the best time to call back. Or, you can leave your name and number, but these are VERY busy people and they may not return your call. Which means, you will have to follow up.

Then, once you get the right man or woman on the phone, explain briefly who you are and ask flat out if he/she would like to see a copy of your book. If they don't do author interviews, they'll say so. If they do show an interest, then make up the best-looking press kit you can and either mail it to them or, even better, deliver it in person.

Again, I cannot stress enough just how important it is to follow up on those phone calls. Be professional and be polite, but use great persistence! That's what counts in this business, more than anything else. Don't give up until you've gotten a definite "yes" or "no". And even when they agree, be sure you tie down the day and hour to come in.

Once you've obtained an interview, write out some questions for the talk show host to ask you. Usually, they are glad to see them, even if they don't use them all or change the wording around to suit themselves. Seldom will an interviewer have time to actually read your book in advance, so you'll want to do all you can to help your host understand what the book's about.

In any interview, do not wax on in a long-winded bull session about your life and how you came to write the book. That audience will tune out and change channels before you know it. Neither will you want to turn your interview into a carnival-like auctioning off of copies.

Instead, slant your talk in a way that gives the potential reader a *reason* to buy a copy. Everyone understands that you'd like to sell a bunch of books. And you will, by selling the book's benefits.

That potential reader is much more interested in his life than yours. Therefore, you'll want to engage him by addressing *his* problems and *his* needs and how your book will solve some of them. What will the *reader* learn in your book that will be of benefit to *him*? How will it enrich *his* life?

Also, their marketing personnel are usually experts in their field. Once you get them on the phone, ask them for their ideas on how you can improve on your efforts to get the word out on your books. Find out what's happening in the local community and how you might get to be a part of it. Any big, promotional event where the radio-station vans will be should be seen as another possibility for you to set up a table and chair, a stack of books, and hope the disc jockey needs someone interesting to talk to on the air. You might be surprised at how they can help.

Many times, these radio talk shows can be a jumping board onto a major T.V. talk show. These will definitely put the sales of your book through the roof!

Below is a list of publications used by talk show hosts all over the country, in looking for interesting people to interview. Some of them will mention your book simply by sending them a press release and some of them will expect you to buy an ad. Either way, be sure to contact them and all radio stations in your area. Find out what their requirements are and make your decision at that time on what you think you can afford.

Newsmaker Interviews
8217 Beverly Boulevard
Los Angeles, CA 90048
(213) 655-2793 Fax: (213) 275-2602

Radio-TV Interview Report
Bradley Communications,
135 E. Plumstead Avenue
PO Box 1206
Lansdowne, PA 19050
(215) 259-1070 Fax: (215) 284-3704

Spotlight
PO Box 51103
Seattle, WA 98113

Below are news services which send their stories out by satellite feed. I would at least send them a press release and/or a copy of a recent review.

News/Broadcast Network
149 Madison Avenue
New York, NY 10016; (212) 889-0888

Jericho Promotions
924 Broadway
New York, NY 10010-6007
(212) 260-3744; Fax: (212) 260-4168

Copley Radio Network,
350 Camino de la Reina, PO Box 190
San Diego, CA 92112
(619) 293-1818 (800) 445-4555

R & R (Radio & Records)
Don Waller, Senior Editor
1930 Century Park West
Los Angeles, CA 90067;
(310) 553-4330 Fax: (310) 203-9763

Talkers
Mona Lipschitz, Sources Editor
Goodphone Communications
PO Box 60781
Longmeadow, MA 01116
(413) 567-3189 Fax: (413) 567-3168

• TV TALK SHOWS

To be totally honest, it's hard to get onto the big shows such as *Oprah*, or *The Today Show*. But it certainly doesn't hurt to try. The local talk-shows, such as those in Seattle, may be easier. And if you interest a local affiliate station, it could lead to some notice from the big networks. Especially if your book speaks to any current issue. A press kit which includes a good news-release, a book and a cover letter explaining why you think they might find your book of interest just might work. You never know in this business who the next celebrity is going to be.

• MORE ABOUT PUBLIC SPEAKING AND PROMOTING YOUR WRITING CAREER

Consider the idea of doing some public speaking, starting at the local level in the community where you live. Offer to do a short reading of your books at local events and festivals. At first, you probably won't be offered any payment other than a chance to sell copies of your book afterwards. Later on, once you've gotten to be better known and have perfected your talk into a viable commodity, you can demand a fee.

Once the plans for your appearance are confirmed, send a news release to any and all newspapers, radio stations, and T.V. stations in the area. Tell them who you are and what you'll be doing. Be sure to invite the reporters to come. You'll be amazed when some of them actually show up and make a point of meeting you and mentioning your work in their media. It's great publicity and it's all free.

A friend of mine, Mark Ortman, author of *A Simple Guide to Self-Publishing*, has made a second career in the business of self-publishing and public speaking. Seldom does a writing or bookselling conference go by, but this hard-working entrepreneur is teaching classes and giving lectures on how to do just exactly what he is doing.

What he has to say about his adventures in the field of self-publishing is quite an eye-opener!

"I self-published more out of necessity than choice. Looking back, I'm glad I did. Having control over the destiny of the book(s) was far more important than turning it over to a someone else. Whose vision is it anyway! What I learned was that publishing is a business and writing is an art, thus ... to dream with my eyes open, not closed. The result is that I am writing, publishing, and promoting my own books full time."
— Mark Ortman, Author
Now That Makes Sense!,
So Many Ways To Say Thank You
Wednesday's Dream
A Simple Guide To Self-Publishing.

Well, there it is. I've imparted every bit of knowledge, every hint, and every one of my secrets in how to self-publish, promote, and market a book successfully. The only thing left to say is that I wish you all the luck in the world and truly hope that your book becomes the biggest bestseller ever!

FLYING SWAN PUBLICATIONS
ORDER FORM

Did you borrow this book? Find it in the library? Like to give one as a gift? Would you like to have it autographed? If so, send name you'd like to have mentioned along with payment and order form. Special discounts for quantity purchases.

Don't have time to enter the addresses into your database? These addresses, chapters four thru seven, are now available on disks, ready for immediate use. This is not a mailing list, but yours to keep and use, again and again. Simply fill out the form below, adding whether you prefer Microsoft Word or Word Perfect.

Questions can be directed toward Ruth Raby Moen at (306) 856-5320.

Send order to: **Flying Swan Publications**
                  P.O. Box 46
                  Sedro-Woolley, WA 98284

Make checks payable in U.S. funds to Flying Swan Publications.

For 4 books or less, include $2.50 shipping and handling. For more than 4 books, freight pre-paid.

Qty.	Name of book	Price each	Tax	Total Per Book	Total Amount
____	*Self-Publishing Can Be Profitable*	$ 17.49	1.36	18.85	_____
____	Computer Disk w/Addresses (Check one: ☐ Microsoft Word ☐ Word Perfect)	$125.00	9.75	134.75	_____
____	*Only One Way Out*	$ 7.95	.62	8.57	_____
____	*Deadly Deceptions*	$ 7.95	.62	8.57	_____
____	*Hayseeds In My Hair*	$ 12.95	1.01	14.93	
				Shipping ($2.50)	_____
				TOTAL	_____

Please print your complete mailing address below:

Name: _____

Organization or Company: _____

Address: _____

City, State, Zip _____

Phone number: (   ) _____

FLYING SWAN PUBLICATIONS
ORDER FORM

Did you borrow this book? Find it in the library? Like to give one as a gift? Would you like to have it autographed? If so, send name you'd like to have mentioned along with payment and order form. Special discounts for quantity purchases.

Don't have time to enter the addresses into your database? These addresses, chapters four thru seven, are now available on disks, ready for immediate use. This is not a mailing list, but yours to keep and use, again and again. Simply fill out the form below, adding whether you prefer Microsoft Word or Word Perfect.

Questions can be directed toward Ruth Raby Moen at (306) 856-5320.

Send order to: **Flying Swan Publications**
P.O. Box 46
Sedro-Woolley, WA 98284

Make checks payable in U.S. funds to Flying Swan Publications.

For 4 books or less, include $2.50 shipping and handling. For more than 4 books, freight pre-paid.

Qty.	Name of book	Price each	Tax	Total Per Book	Total Amount
____	*Self-Publishing Can Be Profitable*	$ 17.49	1.36	18.85	_____
____	Computer Disk w/Addresses (Check one: ☐ Microsoft Word ☐ Word Perfect)	$125.00	9.75	134.75	_____
____	*Only One Way Out*	$ 7.95	.62	8.57	_____
____	*Deadly Deceptions*	$ 7.95	.62	8.57	_____
____	*Hayseeds In My Hair*	$ 12.95	1.01	14.93	
				Shipping ($2.50)	_____
				TOTAL	_____

Please print your complete mailing address below:

Name: _____

Organization or Company: _____

Address: _____

City, State, Zip _____

Phone number: (   ) _____

– NOTES –

– NOTES –

– NOTES –

– NOTES –